KIRABO

*a journey of
faith, love + adoption*

KVETA ROSE

For more information, visit kirabobook.com or email info@kirabobook.com.

The following story depicts one person's journey with international adoption, but does not represent a typical process and is not intended to be a reference or guide to those interested in pursuing adoption. For more information, please see the Resources section at the back of this book.

To protect the privacy of certain individuals, names and identifying details have been changed, and any persons who appear in this book under their real names have given their consent.

Edited by Keri Haywood
Book design by Ariana Bissky
Cover design & photo by Aaron Rose
Photos on page 368 courtesy of Tandela Castilla; used by permission

ISBN 978-1-500266-41-7

To my husband, Aaron

CONTENTS

AUTHOR'S NOTE

I HAD VERY little knowledge of the specific details involved in this miraculous journey of faith, love, and adoption when, in 2008, I nervously asked Tandela, one of my closest friends from university, if I could write down her and Mark's story. I had never aspired to write a book and knew nothing about putting together a biography. All I knew was for the entire year prior, I could not shake the feeling that this was a story to be shared with others, and I felt God was leading me to play a role in sharing it. Tandela's response, which she records in the foreword to this book, both encouraged and affirmed this call.

Over the next four years I grew to know Tandela (who is usually called Tandy by close friends and family) and Mark's story very intimately. I made a number of trips from Vancouver to Calgary, and in interview after interview Tandy allowed herself to be vulnerable, openly sharing the various moments of joy and sorrow that form this incredible narrative.

I remember the day in Calgary when she opened up her precious blue folder, which you will read about. I scoured through the various legal documents, ensuring the dates presented in the book were accurate. You will encounter many of these very documents and letters as you read through the book.

In May of 2011, I traveled to Uganda in order to conduct firsthand research that I believed was necessary to provide accurate descriptions of the events that took place and the relationships Tandy and Mark formed there. I was privileged to visit the orphanage where she volunteered, meet the housemothers who cared for Mark as a baby, and interview Sharon, a friend who supported Tandy and helped her at many crucial stages of the adoption process. I visited the servants' quarters where Tandy lived, as well as the courthouse, various government offices, and the hospital that Tandy and Mark frequented. I even stayed at the same hostel in Kampala as her. This was all done with the intention that the scenes be described with as much realistic detail as possible.

The words on these pages have been formed from interviews with Tandy, her loving family, and other individuals key to the story, with the aid of original emails, letters, legal documents, and research gathered from my trip to Uganda. The characters in the book are all based on specific people, with the exception of the director of the orphanage, Margaret, who is an amalgamation of two different women who served in this position over the four years in which this story takes place. Most people's names and individual characteristics have been changed to provide anonymity, and consent has been granted by those whose names have not been changed. Much of the dialogue is based word for word on conversations Tandy vividly remembers, and some dialogue has been constructed to allow for specific and necessary details to be brought to life in the telling of the story.

The events in this book are relayed in the order in which they occurred with the exception of Chapter One, a fictionalized scene in which Mark is found in the latrine. While we know the name of the town where Mark was discovered, we do not know the location of the pit latrine or the exact circumstances that surround his discovery. I began the story this way to help the reader understand the surreal circumstances surrounding Mark's rescue, and to make the point that God's miraculous hand was upon Mark far before Tandy came into his life.

Kveta Rose
November 2013

FOREWORD

I have found the paradox, that if you love until it hurts,
there can be no more hurt, only more love.

—Mother Teresa

FAITH AND OBEDIENCE did not always come easily for
me. Although I always seemed to have a strong sense
of social justice and "fairness," thanks in large part
to my parents, I never quite understood the connection between genuine faith and action until my early
twenties.

I remember in the summer before my last year of
university being invited to a leadership conference by
my pastor. On the final night of the conference, the

worship band began to sing a song with lyrics based on verses from Isaiah 6. Isaiah hears the voice of the Lord saying, "Whom shall I send, and who will go for me?" and in response Isaiah cries out, "Here I am! Send me."

As I was belting out that last phrase, "Here I am! Send me," I felt a stirring in my soul and knew that God was going to take me up on that. I couldn't sing something like that with my whole heart and expect God to just sit back and ignore it, could I? Almost exactly one year later, I found myself boarding a plane to Uganda, East Africa. Little did I know that those naïve yet genuine words would be the green light God needed to take me, flip me around, and change my life forever.

Years later when my good friend Kveta approached me about writing a book highlighting the journey that God took me on during that time, I had that same stirring. I had been approached about that possibility before, but had never received peace about it until that moment. I knew Kveta's heart for God, in addition to the genuine and caring relationship she had with me. This meant I could not only trust her with my heart, wounds, and vulnerabilities, but also those of my precious family. I knew that Kveta would tell this story from the heart of a servant, a heart that desires nothing more than for God's character and grace to be revealed in these pages, a yearning for people to know of God's goodness and the way he patiently guides those whom he has called.

I can say with a heart of true admiration and gratitude that Kveta has accomplished just that. Through her gentle and heartfelt writing, she has brought to life a story that speaks of God's divine purpose and his ability to turn the ordinary into something miraculous and extraordinary. He is truly a God who loves and knows his people intimately, and it is my prayer that you see that for yourself in these pages. This is not my story; this is God's story. I am just blessed that he used me.

Tandela Castilla
August 2012

KIRABO

CHAPTER ONE

March 2003, Makindye, Uganda

H E DRAGS the yellowing handkerchief across his forehead. His perspiration is only partially due to the intense noonday sun overhead; there is another reason he is sweating. It is the same reason he is unconsciously grinding his teeth, the same reason his knuckles look starkly white against the dark hands that tightly grip his steering wheel. He is dreading the scene that awaits him.

As a police officer, he has responded to a call like this only once before, and it did not turn out well. His mind turns over those events as the dirt road crunches beneath the tires. He makes a left turn toward the taxi park and passes a field. A group of young boys, probably too poor to attend school, are passing the time playing soccer. Their shrieks of joy conflict with the cry of pain that alerted the panicked call to the police station. He wonders, *Aren't social workers better equipped to handle such situations?*

The expansive dirt field, which serves as a meeting spot for buses and taxis, comes into view. He is struck by how suddenly the scene seems dominated by three contrasting colours: the bright reddish-brown dirt of the ground, the vibrant green vegetation along the side of the road, and the deep blue sky that stretches on forever.

The tired brakes squeal as the car pulls to a stop. A small pack of onlookers have gathered. Nearing the crowd on foot, the officer retrieves a pad of paper and pen from his shirt pocket. He will need to record notes as quickly as possible. Two older women dressed in plain but brightly coloured t-shirts and loose flowing cotton skirts wring their well-worn hands. They were likely on their way home from a morning's work of cleaning and washing clothes. Three young men, their days free of employment, huddle together, talking in animated tones. A mother with two young boys, a basket at her feet indicating that she was on her way back from the local market, is unable to hold back her emotion at the scene before her and silently sobs while patting her boys' shoulders at her side. *Where is my partner? He should be here by now.*

The officer can now distinguish specific words from the constant hum of speculation. Even though most of the individuals saw his car pull up, they continue to speak among themselves, avoiding eye contact with him.

"...was walking past..."

"...and listened again. A small cry..."

"...followed the noise..."

"...shivering, shaking. He had nothing but a thin blanket."

"...left in the latrine."

"All night? Days? We will never know for sure."

"A boy. Yes, alive. But for how long?"

"Where is the baby?" the officer demands, letting himself hope for a brief minute that the last comment is true, that the baby is still alive.

Rickety stairs lead from the latrine's brick foundation up to the small wooden shack that houses the opening of the pit. The officer is no stranger to latrines; they are, after all, the only public toilets available to the people of Makindye, a small town outside of Kampala. The ground inside is nothing but a slab of cement with a large hole in the middle. The depth of the pit depends on the last time it was emptied. It could be anywhere from three to six feet deep. Swarms of flies dart in and out of the pit, feasting on the excrement below.

One wants to spend as little time as possible in such places. The odour is strong, and germs are everywhere. The thought of a baby lying in the darkness below, hidden in filth, is so disturbing he is forced to grip his hand over his mouth, fighting his body's urge to vomit. The toxic gases produced by the excrement in the latrine are powerful enough that in hours they could suffocate a baby to death. It can't be true that this baby is still alive.

Behind him, the bystanders move aside as an old woman, her shoulders permanently hunched over by time, makes her way forward. A white scarf covers her head. She wears a yellow and green floral dress that, though faded from many days under the sun, alludes to the care she takes in her appearance. In her lean yet strong arms, arms that have likely held numerous children and grandchildren, she cradles a newborn baby.

The crowd quiets. The officer turns, grimacing in anticipation of what he will see. Approaching cautiously, he peers down at the bundle, his eyes squinting to make out the baby's facial features. The infant is only slightly larger than the officer's fist. His tiny eyes are squeezed shut and his small hands are clenched at his chest. On the baby's chest, a layer of excrement has been wiped away during the rescue, exposing a patch of skin. Though it is coated in a film of greying vernix caseosa, the officer can see a tiny rib cage protruding below. Six inches of grey umbilical cord extend from his minuscule belly button. His lips are blue. He is not moving.

Holding his breath, the officer lowers his face within inches of the baby's, trying to determine whether the newborn is indeed still breathing.

This can't be.

He stares again.

But it is.

He detects a faint rising and falling of the chest. This baby, against all odds, is still alive. This tiny, naked boy has been alone and exposed in a pit latrine for a day, or maybe more, and here he is, fighting for air. Fighting for life.

You don't put someone in a pit latrine so that they will be found.

It is nothing other than a miracle that this child has been rescued. By God's grace, a pair of hands reached down into the dark and filthy pit and raised this baby boy into the light.

And it will take nothing less than a miracle for him to survive.

CHAPTER TWO

October 2003, Jinja, Uganda

I **STAND OUTSIDE** the gated entrance of the orphanage, taking a minute to inhale the sweet aroma from the surrounding foliage laced with smoke from outdoor cooking fires. Shouts from a soccer field across the road mingle with the sounds of birds singing to one another perched high in eucalyptus trees.

Standing on my tiptoes, I crane my neck to see inside. Like many homes and buildings in Jinja, the grounds are lined with a tall security fence. I catch a glimpse of three little children on a swing set, their tiny legs working hard as they reach for the sky. A young man, likely the orphanage's guard, opens the gate slightly and sticks out his head.

"Can I help you, Miss?" he asks me. He wears a baggy dark blue cotton shirt and khaki trousers. His head is shaved, drawing attention to his large almond-shaped eyes.

"I was hoping I could come in and see the children's home,"* I reply. "I'm looking for a place where I can volunteer."

He opens the gate and leads me inside. Immediately I am swarmed by a flurry of affectionate little bodies. Giggles of delight escape their lips as they playfully compete with one another to wrap their arms around me. Not a hint of shyness accompanies the sweaty and sticky hands that now cling to my own. Unashamed, these children shower me, a stranger who has entered their midst only moments ago, with love.

The property seems large compared to other orphanages I have visited. The main building is painted a pale pink. Protective white bars cover all the windows, and the yard is lined with four-foot-high cinder blocks, from which iron bars protrude another four feet into the sky. Bright green vines wind up the bars, softening

---

* *Children's home: The term commonly used in Africa for an orphanage.*

an otherwise severe perimeter. A slight breeze ripples the leaves of an African tulip tree, its branches ripe with reddish-orange flowers. The tree casts a shadow over one corner of the grounds, where several children are gathered to avoid the heat.

I am here to stay. This sounds ridiculous, for I have not even spoken to any of the staff. But there is no mistaking the overwhelming sense of peace I am experiencing at this very instant. After six weeks of unrest since my arrival in Africa, I feel I've found the place God had in mind for me all along. The path getting here was by no means straight, but God has led me all the same. He just threw a few blind turns into the route so I would know for sure that this journey was his doing and not mine.

WHEN I PLANNED my trip to Uganda, I didn't anticipate that I would find myself hitch-hiking in and out of villages, searching for an orphanage where I could be of help. My intention had been to spend six months with a particular family in Mbale, one hundred thirty kilometres northeast of Jinja, but upon my arrival, I realized that a massive misunderstanding had taken place. Well, it was massive from my point of view at least. I was under the impression that I was going to be spending all of my time in Mbale working on the front lines at the orphanage the family oversaw. However, this family was under the impression that I would spend all of my time helping them find overseas funding for the orphanage. The orphanage that, unbeknownst to me, had yet to be built. Because I had been in touch with this family via email for months prior to even arriving in Uganda, I had let myself become invested in their vision to serve the children of Uganda through an orphanage. But when I learned my involvement would not be "hands on" like I had expected, my heart sank. There wasn't a big difference between these two roles from the family's point of view: both served to aid children in need. But for me, having dreamed of working day in and day out with children, such news was disappointing.

I spent four weeks in Mbale, but no matter how hard I tried I could not get excited about spending my days in front of a computer writing grant proposals. Was this why God had brought me to Uganda?

During those four weeks I prayed over and over for discernment on whether God wanted me to stay with this family. As the days passed, the restless feeling in my soul that God had something different in mind only grew stronger. After explaining my feelings to this family that I had grown to love dearly, I began to explore other volunteer opportunities with their support.

In the last week of my search I visited six orphanages, including one specifically for HIV-positive children and three aiding internally displaced population (IDP) camps. At each location the children were heartbreakingly friendly, yet not a single place resonated with me in the way I expected it should. I thought I would know for sure which one was to be "the one," and that I would experience some kind of chemical spark or leap of the heart when I found the right fit. Was I being too picky? Then, two days later, my friends Peter and Mary-Anne told me I should go to Jinja and visit the orphanage from which they had adopted two girls.

And here I am.

A TALL, LEAN Ugandan woman, who looks to be in her mid-forties, makes her way toward me. Her dark hair is pulled back into a short ponytail, emphasizing her high cheekbones. The small scar on her right cheek turns into a dimple when she smiles at me. She holds a baby girl who is hooked up to an oxygen tank, from which a tube winds around her and trails behind them. The woman shifts the baby in her arms so she can shake my hand.

"Hello and welcome. My name is Margaret." Her fingers, though slim, firmly grasp my own in a warm handshake.

"And I'm Tandela. Thank you for letting me come in." I explain to Margaret that I have traveled here from Canada and am looking to help out at the children's home for a few months.

"I'd be happy to show you around," Margaret replies. "We are always looking for help." She hands off the baby to another worker and unwinds herself from the oxygen tube wrapped around her waist with a gentle chuckle.

"Please, after you," she says, motioning toward the front door. As we enter the building, she tells me that the home, caring for fifty-four children who are four years old and under, is well over capacity. Fifteen of them are babies ranging from newborn to six months, twenty are six months to a year old, and the eldest nineteen are between one and four years old.

Margaret takes me into the room where the oldest children sleep. There are four small bunk beds, which means that every bed sleeps at least two children. I cannot help but notice that the sheets are stained yellow from constant bed-wetting. In response to my inquiry of how long the home has existed, Margaret informs me that it was founded eight years ago by a Christian woman from America.

"She meant for it to be a place where the most destitute babies could be cared for," Margaret shares, explaining that upon arriving here, most babies have either malaria, AIDS, tuberculosis, or measles, are literally starving, or are suffering the effects of being born prematurely. "We are able to help a number of them if we can get the right medicine, but some we cannot help, and they stay here for a short time until they pass away. It's better than the alternative," she says, her eyes wide with compassion. "In their dying days we are able to provide the little ones with reassurance that they are loved and wanted. And they do not die alone."

I continue peppering her with questions, my excitement growing with every second. Unlike the previous places I visited, I want to know absolutely everything about this place. Margaret describes the various scenarios that have caused these children to be brought here. Many parents have died from AIDS or other diseases, or perhaps the father died and the mother, sick herself, is unable to care for her children and has no family to rely on for help. Sometimes the mother is very young, a victim of rape, or too mentally unstable to care for a baby. In some tribes the shame of having a baby out of wedlock is so strong that a family will force the woman away in order to save face. And if the child is a result of rape or incest it is viewed by some tribes as cursed. A cursed child is not allowed to stay in the village, and his or her mother and father will be exiled if they are discovered.

I inquire about who brings the children to this safe haven if there are no parents. Margaret informs me that the babies who are abandoned are often found by strangers who generally alert the police. Common places for babies to be found are on top of garbage bins or on the side of the road. They are usually left in locations where they will be easily spotted. Most of the time the mothers of abandoned children will give birth in secret, but on occasion a woman will give birth in a hospital and disappear shortly after, leaving the baby behind. Margaret leads me into a room that looks to be her office.

"We've even had babies brought here that were found floating in baskets in the Nile River. More often than not it is a baby girl that has been abandoned, but we do have many boys here as well." She nods to a chair beside her desk. "Please, Tandela, have a seat and rest your feet. We will get to know each other a little, then I'll finish showing you around. That sound okay?"

Her chair creaks slightly as she takes a seat. On her desk sits a computer, two framed photos, a desk lamp, and a tall stack of papers. To one side is a window, and the other is taken up by a large filing cabinet, likely containing any and all information to be found on the children here. Behind her desk on the wall is a drawing with the words "We love you Mommy Margaret" scrawled in childlike handwriting.

"Have you volunteered in an orphanage before?" she inquires.

"Yes," I reply. "Beginning when I was ten years old."

WHEN I WAS ten years old my family moved to the Philippines for a year and a half while my dad worked there as a physician. Not long after we settled in, my older sister, Kirsten, and I began helping out at a nearby orphanage once a week. My brother, Nathan, was a boisterous five-year-old at the time, and therefore too young to join us. He spent his days at home, enjoying some elusive one-on-one time with Mom. My parents created this arrangement because they thought it would provide an opportunity for Kirsten and me to have our eyes opened, independent of adult agendas, to the reality of how many children in the world live.

I found the first few visits to the orphanage quite distressing. The environment was unlike anything I had ever experienced, for I could not look anywhere without being overwhelmed by the staggering number of basic needs the children lacked on a daily basis. They needed more care, more food, more clothing, and more love. Many of the children had severe disabilities, and there wasn't nearly enough staff there to tend to them all. Unlike my sister, who shows affection with ease, the thought of touching the children also made me very uncomfortable. I didn't know what to do with them. What if I accidentally hurt one of them?

It was also unnaturally quiet, considering the number of babies that lay in the beds lining the white concrete walls. I later learned that the eerie quiet of the babies was, in fact, because the babies had come to realize that crying did not result in anyone coming to help them; they had been nurtured not to cry, trained from birth that crying is a waste of effort. No one is able to respond because the orphanage is under-staffed.

I clearly remember the first child I finally held, a little girl. When I picked her up I noticed that her legs were covered in a bumpy, red rash. Looking down, I saw that she had been sitting on the ground in a mess of her own feces and urine. All of a sudden I was overcome by a deep, weighty sadness. I think it was the first time that I had experienced true sorrow.

When we said goodbye on our last day, the orphanage was no longer quiet. In fact, it had not been quiet for quite some time. With each day that we visited, we all laughed more, sang more, and grew to be just plain noisy. A once painfully quiet orphanage was now full of the sounds of kids being kids.

Something changed inside me during that trip. The memories come flooding back whenever I pause to look at the Philippine items hanging on the wall of my parents' dining room, including a muslin drum and a tool used for rice winnowing. Hanging next to these are other relics from my parents' travels, including instruments from Nepal, an Inuit seal-skinning tool from the Rankin Inlet, and bells from South Africa. And then there is the wedding photo of my parents, who are dressed head to toe in traditional South African dress.

From a young age, this wall kindled in me a curiosity about other countries and cultures. Rather than making these faraway places seem like distant foreign lands, they made me feel connected to them. I always felt particularly drawn to Africa. When we were growing up, Mom and Dad often spoke about their time as physicians in South Africa. That is where they fell in love, working in the same mission hospital. Though they had both graduated from medical school at the University of Alberta, they had separately chosen to spend time in South Africa. That is where my name is from: Tandela means "love" in one of the South African dialects. Maybe that is also why I've always felt a connection to this vast and distant continent. Because, in a way, our family began in Africa.

As a teenager I was desperate to see Africa for myself. I got my first opportunity when, at seventeen years old, I signed up for a trip to Ghana with a group called Volunteers for Peace. I saw this trip as being a bit of a test for me. Had I made up a passion for Africa in my head? Was I to learn I had romanticized going there, or was I genuinely drawn there by seeds sown long ago? Was this a mere interest or something more, perhaps a divine calling?

The trip began with me flying by myself from Canada to Ghana and on arrival being stranded at the airport in Accra when the people who were supposed to pick me up were nowhere to be found. My mom immediately regretted her decision to let her teenage daughter travel so far by herself.

"Tandela, we must have been crazy to let you go!" my mom said over the phone shortly after I had arrived. It had taken a fair amount of convincing for my parents to say yes to the trip. My dad, being more of a dreamer and visionary, was the first to give his consent after a period of constant coaxing. My mother, the more practical one, held out longer with very strong hesitations. I was the youngest participant in the group, and most of the others were at least twice my age. And I wouldn't have the chance to meet anyone else on the team before arriving in Ghana. But Kirsten, going into her second year of studies at the University of Calgary, was supportive, knowing that once I had set my mind on something it was almost impossible to talk me out of it. Nathan, on the other hand, was too young to really understand what the big deal was about and, at just twelve years of age, was more concerned about winning his next hockey game.

A teenager at the time, I was deeply affected by how dealing with death and dying on a daily basis shaped the Ghanaians' perception of life. I found people lived with a vibrancy and fervour that we lacked back home, where living to old age was seen more as a right than a gift. I saw firsthand how life expectancy was indeed one of many ethnographic factors that influenced Ghanaian culture.

The first sub-Saharan African nation to gain independence, Ghana is generally recognized as a peaceful country. Unlike many neighbouring countries, Ghana was not experiencing civil war or post-war conflict during the year I was there. Despite this, the average Ghanaian lived to only fifty-six years old. This was because Ghana was at the height of fighting a different type of war, a different type of violence: HIV. In the town where I was staying, Wa, I learned that approximately one in three men were infected with HIV.

My trip to Ghana not only gave me confidence in my ability to travel alone, but it also quickly melted away any notion I had of the "great white hope." This term has been coined from decades of Westerners traveling to Africa with the misconception that their presence was somehow going to result in bettering or improving the lives of native Africans. I quickly realized that it is often the other way around.

When I arrived, I was determined to have an effect, to do something really worthwhile for a change. And what did I do? I helped build a bathroom. *Yes, I really shook up the village,* I think wryly to myself as I reflect back on my time there. Yet in the end, my fondest memories of that summer had nothing to do with plumbing;

rather, they were of my time spent at an orphanage and a school for deaf children.

Upon returning to Canada, it was difficult for me to articulate my experience. Because of their time in South Africa, Mom and Dad understood the challenge of trying to process and adjust to the differences between the Ghanaian culture I had become accustomed to and my Canadian culture back home. There were many stories I wanted to share with my siblings and friends, and yet the words and images I chose disappointed me. It was as though I was trying to provide details of the colours and grandeur of the Sistine Chapel to someone who had never even heard of it.

Regardless, the trip also served to deepen the attachment I felt to Africa. I still didn't understand why I felt this way or what this meant for my future, but I knew without a doubt that the trip had changed me forever.

"WE WOULD BE more than happy to have you help us out, Tandela," Margaret states when I finish sharing my story. "We are always in desperate need of more hands. Especially when it comes to the babies. They need more attention than we can possibly give." She exhales a weighty sigh. "We are maxed out. But what can we do? The babies keep showing up and we can't turn them away. There is nowhere else for them to go."

I ask Margaret how many staff work at the home, curious to learn about the others who dedicate their love and time.

"Let's see," Margaret begins to count on her fingers. "I think each day we have about five house-mothers, two laundry staff, one or two cooks, and a driver." Margaret goes on to explain that the staff do not live at the home. Rather, those who have families nearby live with them, and the women who come from villages farther away sleep in staff quarters and travel home to their children when they have a day off. I learn that the women who look after the children are called housemothers because they are considered the "mothers of the house."

"That's why the children call me Mommy Margaret," she says.

Margaret suggests we continue our tour of the or-phanage. As she rises from her chair, she calls out to a young woman in the hallway outside.

"Sharon! I'd like you to meet someone."

A young woman rushes in wearing a bright red shirt and blue capri pants, gently smiling at me. Right away my eyes are drawn to her welcoming smile and warm brown eyes. Her hair is piled on top of her head, partly covered by a blue bandana. Margaret introduces us and explains that Sharon helps out at the orphanage mostly on the weekends and in the evenings after school. I notice that her pants are dusted with small handprints, evidence of the fun she has been enjoying with the children outside.

"I don't know what we would do without Sharon," Margaret admits with deep gratitude.

"Tandela," Sharon says thoughtfully, almost under her breath. "What a pretty name." She then politely excuses herself, explaining that she needs to return to the yard to supervise the children. Once Sharon downs the rest of her water and hurries out into the sun, Margaret tells me Sharon is only in her teens. I am a little surprised because she carries herself with the maturity and grace of a grown woman.

To my relief, Margaret suggests I leave my backpack in her office for the rest of the tour. It holds all of my belongings, including my sleeping bag, and I am more than happy to give my shoulders and back some respite. I follow Margaret down the hall, visiting the remaining bedrooms, the kitchen, and the dining area. Eventually we come to the last room, one tucked away at the back of the building. It is where the orphanage keeps all their donated items. The room is cluttered beyond belief. Upon closer inspection I find that most of the boxes are crammed to the brim with clothes as well as medications from overseas, most of which have expired.

"We are so grateful for all of these supplies," Margaret says, "but it is difficult to stay on top of keeping everything organized. It has been on my list of things to do," she admits, "but I just haven't been able to get to it. Something more urgent always comes up."

Margaret tells me that I can sleep in here while I look for a place to rent in Jinja. "You will just have to rearrange things a bit to fit a mattress on the floor," she says. The humour of her understatement is not lost on me.

Margaret invites me to stay for dinner, which is being served in just a few minutes. Knowing I will have only an hour or two of daylight after dinner to clear some space on the floor in the back room for my sleeping bag, I hurry through my meal of bean stew and matoke.* When I finally settle in for the night, I feel cramped and claustrophobic, not to mention exhausted. And yet, I have a great sense of peace that I am exactly where God wants me to be.

---

* *Matoke: Boiled mashed banana.*

Thank you, Lord. I am able to dwell on these words for only an instant before immediately drifting into a deep sleep.

AFTER TWO FULL days of sorting and organizing, the room is finally in order. The medicines that are dangerously past their expiry dates have been thrown out, and I've labeled and rearranged the remainder. I survey the room and can't help but feel a strong sense of satisfaction at what I've been able to accomplish. But more than anything, I am excited. Beginning tomorrow morning, all of my time will be spent with the children. I can't wait.

I hear the day-cook bustling around the kitchen, putting away the last of the dinner dishes. I decide to help myself to a cup of tea before snuggling into my sleeping bag with my Bible and flashlight. As I walk toward the kitchen, I hear a knock at the door.

It is eight o'clock, an unusual time for a visitor to arrive. All the day-shift workers have left, leaving only a few staff here. Being in close proximity, I am the first to the door. I open it to find a young woman no more than twenty years old. Tied to her back in traditional African style is a baby.

Without hesitation, I invite her in. The woman is

extremely fatigued. The whites of her eyes are blood-shot from lack of sleep, while the skin on her cheeks and hands is cracked and dry, a common sign of de-hydration. I can tell from her distraught expression that she does not speak English. I quickly retrieve the cook from the kitchen, hoping that she will be able to communicate with our visitor.

"I have come from Kitgum and today arrived in Jinja." The cook translates the woman's Luganda for me. Kitgum is located hundreds of miles north toward the Sudanese border. Tears begin to stream from the young woman's face and the cook tenderly helps her into one of the chairs in the dining area. I offer to make some tea, and the cook nods her head in agreement.

I hurry into the kitchen, returning shortly with a mug in one hand and a plate of digestive cookies in the other. I offer both to the young woman, who has now untied her baby from her back and is cradling him in her arms. She breaks off a small portion of cookie with one hand and dips it into the tea. She blows softly to cool it and holds it to her baby's lips.

"I have no more milk," she confesses shamefully. "He is starving because I have no milk."

I don't have to ask why this woman's breast-milk

has dried up. Her emaciated features say it all. Like her baby, she is starving.

"The rebels, they came to my village. I was at the well collecting water. It is a long walk from my home. When I came back I knew something was wrong. It was quiet and there were small fires everywhere. I tried to hide, but they found me. The rebels. They killed everyone in the village. They killed my whole family, my parents, my sister, and my husband. They dragged me over to my family. And they forced me to —" The young woman pauses and looks away from us. "They chose to punish me instead of kill me. They said they would kill my baby in front of me and then me if I didn't do as they said." She closes her eyes, her pain of reliving this moment etched on her face. Her hand intuitively finds her baby's head and gently caresses it. I am unsure which of them needs this loving gesture more. "The rebels, they held a gun to my head and made me eat the flesh of my husband until they were satisfied."

I grip the edge of the table to keep from falling. Taking deep breaths, I try to cast away the overwhelming urge to vomit.

"They laughed as they watched. I was so frightened," she says quietly, her hand shaking as she raises the cup of tea to her lips. "All the food in our village is gone. Stolen. I am left with nothing. And there is nowhere safe up north. The LRA* is kidnapping our children and killing us, wiping out whole villages. I couldn't think of anything to do but travel as far away from there as I could."

I watch as the cook gathers together some food, blankets, and clothes. There is not much else we can do other than give this woman a night's rest and send her on her way in the morning with a little money. We have hardly enough resources to feed our own children.

MY EYES FOLLOW the young woman, her baby tightly swaddled on her back, as she disappears out of sight past the orphanage walls and into the morning sun.

I ask Margaret what will happen to her. She shrugs her shoulders. I can hear the sadness leak out of her lungs as she exhales. She tells me there are IDP camps designed to help people like her, but many of them are in bad shape. Even in the camps, people have been known to die of hunger.

"Joseph Kony, what he is doing, it is practically un-speakable," she declares, a quiet rage in her voice. "And it has been going on far too long." She shakes her head. "Children began to be abducted by his army in 1987."

LRA: Lord's Resistance Army.

"Why?" I ask, stirred with fury. "Why did he choose children? What is he trying to do?"

"Why? He is not the first. The child soldier has existed for many, many years — and not just in Africa. It is for the same reason people all over the world engage in forced child labour. Children are more easily dehumanized than adults. They don't demand pay, they are easy to come by — in Africa at least — and after they have been brainwashed, they are frighteningly loyal and fearless until death. There is nothing more terrifying I can think of than finding myself face to face with a child who has had every ounce of compassion beat out of him." Her shoulders shake, and she subconsciously moves to rub her arms.

Margaret informs me that Joseph Kony is a self-proclaimed spiritual prophet who leads the rebel group known as the Lord's Resistance Army, or LRA. She explains that other than his hatred for the Ugandan president, Yoweri Museveni, and his desire to have him overthrown, Kony has not made his political agenda clear. His army is well equipped, receiving considerable support from the Sudanese government. In recent years, Kony has focused his tactics on maintaining power by terrorizing northern Uganda, plundering and burning entire villages, and abducting children for the purpose of building his army. These children are forced to kill or be killed, and some are sent over the border to Sudan where they are forced to fight against the Sudanese People's Liberation Army. It is nearly impossible to rescue stolen Ugandan children once they are forced over the border because the Ugandan People's Democratic Army is not allowed into Sudan.

Most Ugandans have seen photos in the news regarding Kony's mutilation practices, like how he cuts out people's tongues, entirely slices away their lips, and forces their mouths shut by locking their lips together. Literally. With a padlock. The purpose of these mutilations is to render his victims speechless and ignite such inconceivable fear in the witnesses that they don't dare do or say anything against him and his army.

"I have heard of some of the things that Kony has done to people," I admit with a shudder. "But I had not heard of forced cannibalism."

"Yes. It is evil," Margaret says again, her voice brought low by sadness, almost to a whisper. "We are a strong people and it will not go on forever. I know there are many good people working on it, on ending the war. And we must have hope, right, Tandela? If there is anything God has taught me in my time at the home here, it is that God is good. He is very, very good.

Don't let the evil sins of one man cause you to doubt that truth."

"Come on," she puts her arm around me and squeezes my shoulder. "Let's go inside and be God's hands and feet."

CHAPTER THREE

November 2003, Uganda

A FTER TWO weeks here, I am feeling quite at ease and less and less a stranger to Jinja every day. I find a place to rent relatively quickly. It is a small two-bedroom unit known here as "servants' quarters," which means it was originally built to house the family's domestic workers. For financial reasons, my landlord, an Indian man who spends a lot of time working in Dubai, has cut down on his domestic staff and decided to rent out the extra quarters.

My place is a twenty-five–minute walk from the orphanage and is near a market where I can pick up fruit and vegetables. The kitchen is very basic — there is no stove or fridge — but it has a sink and an area to prepare meals. There are two bedrooms and a bathroom with a toilet and a showerhead. I am really just there to sleep. I leave for the orphanage early in the morning and often do not get home until after nine o'clock at night. My home décor consists of a disheveled bed and a backpack stuffed with clothes.

This morning I leave at seven o'clock, which will put me at the orphanage in time for the beginning of my shift at seven thirty. I've left the windows, which are protected by steel bars, slightly ajar, allowing air to circulate through the house while I am gone. Inside, the curtains flutter momentarily, their bright floral-patterned fabric a pleasant contrast to the drab beige concrete walls.

Tiny flecks of dust twirl in the air behind me as I walk toward the gate. An overlay of cement covers the ground inside the compound, helping to keep the area relatively clear of reddish-brown dust, a trademark of Ugandan soil. A palm tree stands tall amid numerous smaller shrubs lining the private driveway, their purpose much the same: to provide a screen against more dust entering the yard.

I softly close the gate behind me and am at once aware of the familiar sounds of Jinja waking. I can hear chatter from the small outdoor market up the street as women set up pyramids of bright green mangoes, jackfruit, tangerines, pawpaw berries, pineapple, and yellow and green bananas. Car doors slam as people quickly drop off goods they hope will sell by the end of the day. In the distance, a groaning lawnmower competes with the constant din of numerous birds. Someone is building something; the sound of metal hitting metal splices through the air.

A block away from the market a chicken scurries across my path. I can hear the rest of its clan squawking somewhere in the distance. An older man passes me heading the opposite direction, pushing a bicycle laden with cabbages. He is the first man I've seen here with white hair. I walk past a number of homes reminiscent of the prosperity that many Indians experienced in Jinja before Idi Amin's reign.

Uganda is still recovering from the dictatorship of Idi Amin, who during his reign forced tens of thousands of people of non-African descent out of the country and murdered hundreds of thousands of Ugandans. Amin's radical and devastatingly brutal antics left a wake of economic and social ruin. After eight years in power, Amin was driven out of Uganda by the Tanzanian army. Eventually, some refugees who had been forced out returned and, like my current Indian landlords, were able to claim back any property they had owned prior to their forced departure.

The Indian architectural influence is evident in the large wrap-around balconies, white arches and pillars, and numerous decorative trimmings. A number of these homes have been renovated to look new and now house Jinja's rich and elite. However, many continue to erode, leaving only a glimpse of how beautiful they must have been in their prime.

Throughout the properties, large palm trees reach for the sky, their growth unaffected by past economic and political turmoil. A faint rustling is barely audible as a gentle breeze sways the palm fronds back and forth. I pause and turn around, facing the way to Kampala. Various shades of green, more than I could ever imagine, make up the countryside. The massive blue sky hovers above, protectively spreading its wings over everything below.

As soon as I arrive at the orphanage I go straight to the babies' dormitory. The room is overcrowded with what look like tiny bunk beds, but a closer inspection reveals they are actually cribs stacked one on top of the other. Since the number of babies exceeds the number of cribs, two or three babies are sleeping in each crib.

They droop their arms over each other and nestle their heads against each other's backs. They are adorable when sleeping. It is cute to see how they get used to the presence of their bedmates, and yet at the same time it is sad because it's a reminder that not only do these infants not have their own beds, they do not have their own homes or families.

When the babies aren't sleeping, they are most likely crying. Other than sleeping and screaming, they don't do much else, including eating. Having very little appetite is not unusual for babies who have suffered physical abuse, malnutrition, or abandonment. Unfortunately, by not eating well they cease to gain weight as they should. A lack of weight gain, especially for those who are premature or have been severely malnourished, is a great inhibitor to their physical and mental development.

Their dark red faces and trembling lower lips make me want to cry. And I often do. My tears rub off on their cheeks as I hold them, and their runny noses dampen my face in return. And yet the babies are also leaving a different kind of mark on me, one that is not washed off with soap and water at the end of the day. Something is happening within my heart. Every day I feel myself being drawn to them more and more.

This is surprising, seeing as I have never been particularly crazy about babies. In all my past experiences with children, I have always felt more comfortable with the ones who have grown well past the toddler stage. When, on my third day here, Margaret told me she was putting me in charge of the ten sickest children, most of whom are babies, I did my best to talk her out of her decision. But she was adamant. Even though I had no formal medical training, she felt that my undergraduate psychology degree qualified me over everyone else for this monumental task.

This newfound love I feel for the babies, in addition to the toddlers in my care, can only be described as God-given. And I am immensely grateful to God for this. If my heart had not immediately broken for these little ones, I would have asked unapologetically to be reassigned to a different group of children within the first week. I earnestly love them.

But they are absolutely exhausting.

Sadly there just aren't enough arms around to hold them, cuddle them, and reassure them that they are now safe. The poor souls sound like they are in so much pain. And I do not know how to help. They cannot tell me where it hurts. They are so helpless. So fragile. And loud. They cry, usually staring into space and rarely making eye contact. The trauma that many of the babies at the orphanage have suffered in the first weeks and months of their lives greatly affects their ability and desire to respond to simple things such as touch and noise. It is rare that a baby will cuddle with me or acknowledge my presence with a playful coo. *Will this ever change for them?* I wonder.

I recall from a second-year psychology class at university that severe trauma has the capability to permanently alter the brain's chemistry. What has happened to some of these children will haunt them for the rest of their lives. If they have experienced severe injustice at the hands of someone they trusted, it is highly likely they may grow to be distrustful and highly suspicious of others, leading to social isolation and minimal attachment.

The day shift begins with the housemothers transferring the babies from their cribs to the dining area where they are propped up on the floor on a plastic mat. Those that can't hold their heads up sit in a housemother's lap. The toddlers and older children sit by themselves at small picnic tables. Porridge made from millet is dispersed into sippy cups. Spoonfuls of margarine have been added to the porridge to provide the children with much-needed extra calories. The best thing for the babies would be baby formula, but that is far beyond the orphanage's budget. The children must make do with millet.

The sippy cups have the tops cut off to allow the babies to suck out the porridge inside. If a child is able to grasp a sippy cup, he is left to feed himself. Porridge falls to the floor all around me each morning as the babies and toddlers wildly fling their cups in their little hands. No one is spared from getting speckled in porridge. Up and down, up and down they pound their cups with shrieks, looking around to see if they might receive an adult reaction. But those are hard to come by, as the housemothers are busy, running back and forth through the aisles to distribute the food.

How much food actually makes its way into their little stomachs? It is impossible to monitor how much each child actually eats. I wish that I could spend half an hour trying to coax the sickest ones to eat. But I cannot, since to do so would be to neglect the others. I stare at the little faces before me, all smeared with white chunks of creamy millet. I can tell that they don't mind the mess. Their eyes shine bright under dark eyelashes dotted with porridge.

The toddlers around me are too young to understand that their place here is due to a tragic circumstance.

One day they will know this, and they will understand what it means to be an orphan. I long to protect them from the pain this will bring. A sippy cup falls to the floor beside me, narrowly missing my head, and I pick it up. *What is your plan for each of these children God? What will their stories be?* My mind quickly shifts from such thoughts as I focus on frantically trying to help the children finish their porridge.

After breakfast is bathtime. An assembly line of little black bodies covered head-to-toe with varying amounts of food leads into the bathroom. Into the tub of soapy water they go, then into a different tub with rinse water. Once they are rinsed, they are dressed and ready for playtime outside in the courtyard.

It is only nine thirty in the morning, yet to me it feels like the middle of the day, for the last two hours have already been a whirlwind of exhausting activity. Before we bring the children outside, thin foam mats have to be laid over the concrete to provide some cushion for the babies and toddlers as they play. Sharon and I work side by side, laying the mats out with care. Since today is Saturday, Sharon is here for the whole day. Her calm and confident demeanour, along with the interesting conversations we have together, make me look forward to the times she is at the orphanage.

We position the mats in the one corner of the yard that is protected by the large African tulip tree's shadow. Across from us sits a swing set, and tucked against one wall are three tricycles, the favourite toys among the three- and four-year-olds.

"How were your classes this week?" I ask as we carefully fit the last of the mats together. Sharon is in her last year of secondary school. Yesterday, while we were feeding the children dinner, she told me that next fall she is planning on attending university in Kampala. Our conversation got cut short, as they often do around mealtimes, and I never got a chance to ask her if she had a particular program in mind.

"They were okay," she replies. "I have two exams coming up that I really need to do well in because they will influence the mid-year marks that will be on my university application. I am hoping to get an academic scholarship; that is the only way I will be able to afford to attend university."

Sharon continues to live where she grew up, a small and very poor village a half-hour walk from Jinja. After her mother passed away when she was eleven, she moved in with her aunt. Her father still lives in the village, but with another wife.

"Are you interested in a specific program?" The sun

beats down on our faces as we step out from under the shade of the beautiful tulip tree, its branches still heavy with large reddish-orange blossoms.

"Something that will help prepare me to come back to my village and start a children's home. But a home that exists not just for orphaned children to come to, but one that is specifically tailored to children who are struggling with serious physical issues."

There are a small number of children at the orphanage that have been born with special physical needs and others that developed them after birth because of the abuse and neglect they suffered as babies. There is one little girl, Maya, who is three years old, but instead of being able to walk, she can only scoot around on her bum. Her legs are crooked and mangled because of the numerous fractures she sustained as a baby at the hands of her stepmother.

Sharon goes on to tell me that she hopes the credentials she will be able to gain through a university education will help her down the line in getting proper certification and funding for a special needs orphanage.

"There are many organizations with good intentions, and they are doing good things," she acknowledges, "but they don't reside here. They are not Ugandan. It is different." She explains that there is no quick fix for her country, for its problems are complicated. "This is my home, and these are my people. And this is what I believe God wants me to do."

From the first moment I met her, Sharon impressed me with her composure and her grace, speaking with a wisdom beyond her sixteen years. Now I have gained a further glimpse of the courage, tenacity, and hope within her heart. Day in and day out, Sharon faces the suffering and the poverty of the people in her village. She has seen friends and family members die of AIDS, and time and time again she is reminded of the horrific acts being committed in her country's civil war. I have no idea what this must be like.

"How do you stay so optimistic? With all that you have lived through?" I ask, amazed.

Sharon pauses before she responds, leaning back on her heels. Her kind almond-shaped eyes gaze into my own, and yet she seems to be looking at something beyond me, something that I could never see.

"I have lived through great joys as well, Tandela," she reminds me softly, without a hint of condescension in her voice. "When people visit here they think, 'Oh, what a sad state this country is in. I feel so bad for them. What can we do to help them get out of their misery?' But they don't really see inside us, they don't see the resilience of our souls. We know that suffering is a part of life. We expect it. We are not surprised when something bad happens, but it doesn't give us reason to despair. Just because life can be hard here does not mean that life is not very good. And the rest of the world may not know it, but there are many Ugandans who are doing very good things and bringing good change to our country."

Sharon's words speak to an inner fortitude that I have rarely encountered in North America. Her passion for her country is not founded in pride but rather in love and respect for those who call Uganda home. I am deeply humbled by the burden she carries for her country and its children, one that she carries with great joy and conviction. I want to be more like her in this way, and I hope that when I return to Canada my heart will ache more for the many people who live in need around me day after day.

I go inside to gather some children and return with one baby on each hip. Out of the bins come a number of toys, and immediately the babies begin to jostle each other, squirming toward the numerous toy trucks, rattles, and balls that are being dispersed on the mats. The older children enjoy the freedom of the grounds, making up games or taking turns on the swing set and tricycles. Within minutes, everyone seems to be occupied in some way.

Except for one tiny baby.

One little boy, smaller than anyone else, lies motionless on the mat. He is familiar to me, for he is one of the sick babies in my care, and yet I have never seen him so still. *Is he dead?* I can't breathe, and my skin instantly becomes covered in goose bumps. I'm terrified that this little baby has just perished in front of my eyes. And then he blinks. I hardly have time to take a breath when, with great dismay, I watch as an older toddler steps on the baby, determined to secure a toy beyond his reach. And still the baby does not move. Not even a flinch. He lies as motionless as the mat beneath him. Where any other child would have cried out in pain, this baby offers not even the slightest acknowledgment that he has been touched.

I quickly run over and sweep him into my arms, protecting him from the chaos of the other children. His body is frail and his skin is so dry it is painfully cracked and peeling. His beautiful brown eyes, still devoid of expression, are large compared to his tiny face. I gently stroke the tight mound of black curls on his head.

"It's okay, I've got you now," I whisper in his ear. As I hug him, I can feel his little heart beating. Suddenly a fierce longing to protect this child washes over me, and I am stirred with an intense compassion and love for this particular baby. I speak to him again, this time using his name.

"I'm here. I'm here, Mark."

Mark arrived at the orphanage eight months ago when he was only a few days old. He was discovered in the bottom of a pit latrine in Makindye, a small town on the outskirts of the capital city of Kampala. He was covered in excrement and maggots. The physicians at the hospital in Kampala estimated he had been in the pit latrine anywhere from twenty-four to forty-eight hours. The police questioned a number of locals in Makindye, but no one volunteered any information that would help identify the woman who had given birth to Mark.

I walk back to the corner of the yard and sit with Mark in my arms. Sharon makes her way back to the shade and sits down beside us. She nods at Mark with disbelief. "It is a miracle that he was found. And that he was alive," she says, shaking her head. "I don't remember any other child coming here that was found in a pit latrine. Many are found in garbage bins or left on the steps of the orphanage in a blanket. But not pit latrines. Those babies are usually never found."

A lump forms in my throat with the thought of what must have transpired on that day. The words of Joseph in the book of Genesis come to mind, and I am comforted by the truth about God that is made clear in this particular passage. Joseph's brothers sold him as a slave into Egypt out of jealousy. Years later, after Joseph is reunited with them, the brothers throw themselves at his feet, fearing his revenge. In response Joseph tells them, "You intended to harm me, but God intended it for good" (Genesis 50:20).

Against all odds, Mark was found alive. And I choose to have faith that God somehow intends his abandonment for good.

EVER SINCE THE day of the mat incident, I can't help but feel drawn to Mark more and more. I spend every spare minute I have with him. He is the sickest of all the babies at the orphanage, and I have no idea how to help him. The housemothers tell me he has been plagued with infections ever since he was brought to the orphanage as a newborn. He is constantly stricken with diarrhea and vomiting from chronic intestinal issues. Weighing only seven pounds at eight months old, he is dangerously underweight. His entire body looks as though it is suffering from eczema, so I cover it in Vaseline after every bath. I cover his lips too, for they are painfully chapped due to dehydration.

For ten days now, I have rocked him in my arms every night, praying his little body would yield to the sleep he so desperately needs. I recall learning in my undergrad psychology courses that touch is incredibly important and that babies who do not receive enough touch in the first year of their lives can be developmentally stunted or even die from such neglect. So as much as I can, I hold him, I sing to him, and I pray over him. I put my finger in his little palm and long for him to close his fingers over mine, to give some indication that he knows he is being touched.

But Mark does nothing. His eyes are still vacant, his body still unnervingly unresponsive. And yet I am changing. With each hour that I hold him I can feel myself taking on his pain. I begin to stay at the orphanage later and later each night, leaving only when Mark has fallen asleep. I walk home filled with anxiety about his condition. Tonight in particular, I am worried about his right eye. It is becoming increasingly swollen. I toss and turn all night, wondering if things will have improved by the time I arrive in the morning.

As I ENTER the babies' dorm the next morning, I am praying that Mark's eye infection is better. I am still halfway across the room when I know something is seriously wrong. Mark's eye is so swollen that it appears as if an extra head has attached itself to where his right eye should be. Puss is oozing out of it. Mark whimpers as I gently peel his eyelid back to inspect his eyeball. His whimper is promising, because it means he can still feel something. His eyeball is so red it looks like it is on fire. He must go to the hospital immediately.

"Take the orphanage van," Margaret instructs me, placing the keys in my hand. This is the first time I have driven in Uganda, and I feel incredibly disoriented. Driving on the opposite side of the road with the driver's seat on the right rather than on the left is strange, and this is compounded by the fact that I have an infant in my lap. Horns sound from every direction, but I am too focused on looking straight ahead to figure out if they're honking at me. There are no traffic lights to tell me when to go and when to stop.

It is a miracle in and of itself that Mark and I arrive at the hospital inflicted with no worse injuries than when we left the orphanage. The hospital is government-run, which means that people can be treated here free of charge. Because of this, there is a lineup running outside the main doors to the entrance of the driveway. The wait is hours long. Some mothers hold children hooked up to IVs. I have heard stories of children dying while waiting for care, and I pray this will not be the case for us.

I try to feed Mark some yogurt that I brought with us but he refuses to open his mouth. I sway back and forth, cradling him in my arms while he slides in and out of sleep. Every time he wakes it is a relief, for I fear he may fall into a coma. When we finally see a doctor, we are given a topical antibiotic cream with instructions that it be applied daily. I wish they would keep Mark here; I wish there was something they could do for him that would guarantee his health would improve. If only there was some perfect medicine that could take away all the pain brought on by his constant ailments.

I return to my place at two o'clock in the morning after soothing Mark to sleep. It's around dinnertime back in Calgary and I long to get my mom's advice on Mark's condition, so I pick up my cheap cell phone and dial my family's home number. Though my mom's practice now primarily focuses on geriatric care, I know she will be able to offer some helpful instruction on what I can do to help Mark's health improve.

Nathan answers the phone. I haven't spoken with him since the day I left for Uganda, and am still surprised at how deep his voice sounds. While I was away at university, Nathan grew up, and now at eighteen, he is a young man. He asks about Jinja and how I spend most of my time at the orphanage. When I inquire how he is doing and what he has been up to, his answers are short and elusive.

I don't have to ask why he sounds so sad and distant. Two years ago, six of his friends died in a car accident, including his two closest. They were all in the same car, driving back from a summer camping trip in the middle of the night, when the car crashed. Nathan had also planned to go on the trip, but a couple of days prior he ended up getting a new job and had to stay back to work.

His world fell apart after that, and he has been trying to cope with putting the pieces back together ever since. Kirsten and her husband, Kelly, were married shortly after the accident, and in all of their wedding photos Nathan stares gloomily into the camera, his eyes full of grief. Once an outgoing teenager full of enthusiasm, Nathan is now quiet and melancholy.

"How is he doing?" I ask Mom when she comes to the phone.

She tells me that he doesn't talk to her or Dad much. "I think he stays up pretty late and then spends most mornings in bed, trying to sleep," she says. "Your dad and I are trying to be patient and wait this season out," she shares, her voice shaking slightly with emotion. "There is a lot of pain there, and sometimes the only thing that will make it go away is time. I am praying that God would send some sort of mentor into his life. I know Dad and I can't play that role. Nathan wants to keep his distance from us right now. He's still a teenager, and often one's parents are the last people that a teenager wants to confide in."

I hurt for Nathan and all that he is going through. I can only imagine what our parents must feel as they watch him struggle day after day. I pray that when I return home the two of us will be able to spend some quality time together, and that perhaps he'll begin to open up to me. He needs to talk to someone; he needs to let someone in.

"How about you, how are you doing?" Mom asks. I fill her in on what transpired at the hospital today, and how I feel at a loss as to how to help Mark. She listens patiently for me to finish, just as if I were a patient in her clinic.

"He needs an in-depth physical examination, to

start with," she informs me. I tell her that we have a physician coming to the orphanage in a few days to assess the children, in particular the ones in my care as they are the most at risk. She goes on to say that because Mark is severely underweight, coaxing him to eat and drink must continue to be my main focus. She suggests I always have food or a bottle on hand and try at regular intervals to get him to eat. I also need to have him try to drink some water throughout the day, as this will help with his dehydration.

"I know it is so hard to see people so sick, especially a baby," she adds. "If you think his eye infection is getting worse, take him to the hospital immediately. He'll need something stronger than a cream, probably antibiotics through an IV."

I thank Mom for her advice, and promise to call soon with an update. It's now close to three o'clock in the morning, so I set my alarm for six forty-five. But the alarm proves unnecessary, as my mind is far too preoccupied with thoughts of Mark's dire condition to allow my body any rest.

Over the next two days I diligently apply the ointment to Mark's swollen eye, yet am doubtful there has been any improvement. During the entire day he probably only swallows two mouthfuls of food, which he vomits up shortly after. It breaks my heart to see such a tiny baby, hardly able to hold up his head, lurch forward, compelled by the urge to vomit. Mark's skin is still continually dry and cracked, which can only add to his discomfort. There has not been a single day in his life when he has been free of physical suffering. He seems to be fading away, not just physically, but withdrawing from the world as well. Every day he moves less, blinks less, and cries less.

Lord, help this little child.

CHAPTER FOUR

November–December 2003, Uganda

F HE continues in this way, I don't think this little one is going to make it." The physician, a robustly built Ugandan man in his early forties, removes his glasses and wipes his perspiring forehead with a pink handkerchief. "I estimate he will be gone in less than one month."

My heart sinks in my chest. The physician is so calm, his words so matter of fact. But then I guess he sees more death than I could ever fathom.

The physician is from the Holy Cross International

Clinic, and he is at the orphanage to do his semi-annual assessment of the children. As I am responsible for overseeing the ten sickest babies, I have not left the physician's side. He thoroughly checks over each precious child in my care.

"Mark cannot go on surviving in this state," the physician continues. "He is not gaining any weight because of his chronic diarrhea and constant vomiting. And you can tell his immune system is very weak—how often do you say he experiences these eye infections?"

"Every week or so his eye seems to flare up again," I reply.

"How much attention does he get?"

I lift my eyes from Mark to once again face the physician.

"I'm with him whenever I can be," I profess. "I hold him more than I hold any other baby. In the evenings, when the other children go down, I stay here and hold him for hours, trying to get him to sleep. I've been doing this for almost two weeks without any reaction from him," I confide, my head lowering as I admit my failure. "No eye contact, no recognition. Nothing."

The doctor nods. He runs his hand over his head and lets out a deep breath. The wrinkles in his forehead speak to the many dire prognoses he has had to give.

"You are doing everything you can," he reassures

me. "The damage was done long before you met him. It cannot be undone now. If the pain seems to be getting worse, bring him to the hospital and they will give you something to make him more comfortable in his last days."

He tries to reassure me by saying that I am giving Mark the gift of being loved and cared for while he is dying. Yet the truth of the physician's words are like daggers to my heart. Until today, I had refused to entertain the possibility that Mark was dying. I knew he was drastically ill, but I kept telling myself he was going to pull through this rough patch. For if he didn't, I believed my heart would shatter into a million pieces.

After the physician leaves, I rest my head in my hands. I feel helpless in the face of such a dire prognosis. This is not the first prognosis of its kind the home has received, of course. By now, the housemothers are accustomed to having to deal with such news and have learned how to cope with the prediction that a little one in their care is going to die. But I am not prepared for this kind of grief.

After the children are fed dinner and dressed for bed, I try to calm my nerves with a quick breath of fresh air. I stare into the distance where the roads seem to converge and disappear into the massive rolling hills that line the journey to Kampala. For once, the familiar evening song of birds tucked high in the bushy marula trees that line the road do not soothe me. Nor does the sight of the setting golden sun, slightly obscured by billows of smoke winding their way up from outdoor stoves, take my breath away. Today I am immune to the distinctive beauty brought on by dusk. Even the sight of a group of young boys gathering for a game of soccer, full of energy after a day indoors at school, does not make me smile. Mark may never live to play soccer. How is this fair? Try as I might, I cannot stop the tears. The doctor's words haunt me. *He may not even last a month.*

More than two weeks have passed since my heart was pierced by the sight of Mark lying as still as death on the mat. And ever since then I have been praying that God would help him, that God would save his life. In these times of prayer, I have felt God telling me repeatedly that he has brought me into this situation for a reason. But what reason? I don't know why I am so drawn to Mark, but I do know that when I am with him I experience a sense of purpose that defies explanation.

But God, why would you allow me to become so invested in and so attached to this tiny beautiful creation of yours if you are going to take him away? Why, God, have you introduced me to this boy and made me love him? My anger and confusion almost feels overwhelming.

When I finally arrive home late into the night, I sit in my bed, burying my face in my pillow. *God, what is your reason for sending me to this orphanage and placing this dying baby in my care? Why have you allowed me to be drawn to a child who is going to die?* My pillow grows increasingly damp and salty. Every nerve is aware of the silence that surrounds me.

"Lord, can you heal him? Will you help him? What is your will for this little boy?" I cry out.

I am desperate for God's presence in the midst of feeling so alone. I know from past experiences that God can use feelings of loneliness to draw me to him and remind me that he is my Creator, my Almighty Father, and my Saviour. I bury my face, covered in perspiration and tears, in my hands.

"Why have you given me a burden for Mark?" I moan. "Why have you allowed me to love him when you are going to take him away so soon?"

It has likely been happening for weeks now, but I do not clearly hear or understand what is revealed until this very moment, in the midst of my prayers. It doesn't come in the form of a loud booming voice, or even in the form of a whisper. Nonetheless, it is there. A silent stirring in my soul. The unmistakable nudging of God.

Once I recognize this feeling, I hear a soft, gentle voice from somewhere deep within me asking me to look beyond myself. To see beyond my needs and my insecurities into God's perfect love and perfect plan for my life. I am to give more than just my concern and my time to this little child; I am to love him fully and unconditionally, to fight for his survival, and to care for him for the rest of his life.

I am being called to be his mom.

"No way," I say aloud. This is absurd. *Who am I that you would ask this of me? No, no, no.* I am not going to entertain for a minute the idea that my bond with Mark is to be anything more than what it has been to this point. *Okay, God, this is how it is going to be. I am going to look after him when I am at the orphanage, and I will continue to be devoted to him until he passes away.*

That is all.

THREE DAYS AFTER the physician's visit to the orphanage I call my sister. I am a mess and haven't been able to sleep. Ever since that day, I have been wrestling with the absurd idea that it is God's will for me to be Mark's mother.

I call her from my servants' quarters early in the

morning. The connection is bad, full of static.

"Tandy? Is that you?"

"Yes, it's me," I reply, my voice trembling from sudden homesickness at the sound of Kirsten's voice.

"Are you all right? Are you crying?"

"I feel like God wants me to adopt a little boy here, but it doesn't make any sense." The words spill out of my mouth quickly, almost on top of each other.

"Slow down, Tand. I can hardly hear you. Did you say adopt?"

"Yes, but it doesn't make sense." I take a deep breath, trying to steady myself. "I'm single, and I don't have any money. I'm too young. He's not even supposed to live."

Kirsten is my best friend, my rock. Mom and Dad have always gone to church, but I was never interested in going with them. It was only after Kirsten started going to church with friends as a teenager that I began to check it out for myself. In fact, I have often found myself longing for the type of faith with which Kirsten has been gifted. It is as though God created her with a certain sweetness and naïveté that makes believing in the gospel the most natural thing in the world, while others like me are more easily plagued and weighed down by doubt from the brokenness of our world.

Kirsten is more protective of me than anyone else

in my family, and I know that I can count on her to give me wise and honest counsel on this topic. Every day that I am away from her, I know she is praying for me.

I tell Kirsten how Mark came to the orphanage, and how he has been continually ill since the day he was born. I fill her in on what the doctor told me and how I can't shake the feeling that God has given me a fierce love for Mark as part of his bigger plan for me to look after Mark long-term.

"I just don't understand why God would want me to try to do this. I don't even have a clue of how international adoption works."

"Tand, if God wants this to happen he will overcome all barriers."

"But this is adoption. This is a child. This is my life."

Kirsten empathizes with my worries but reminds me that fear can never be an excuse when it comes to choosing whether or not we will be obedient to God. I appreciate the truth of her words, and, like many times before, long to be naturally more optimistic like my sister.

"I wish I could be there with you," Kirsten continues. "I will pray for you. Let's fast and pray together about this over the weekend. Whenever we feel hungry or it is mealtime, we will instead each seek solitude and will pray for God to make his will for this situation known to you. I..."

Click.

"Kir? Kir! Are you there?"

All I can hear is static. The reception has cut out. My sister is gone.

I AM CURLED up in my bed. It is almost nine o'clock on Saturday night. It has been two days since my conversation with Kirsten. I have spent much of the day in prayer. During mealtimes, instead of eating, I have opted to pray and read my Bible. I am reading my way through the Gospels, praying that God will use Scripture to show me what he wants me to do.

I get to John 14:18 and read, "I will not leave you as orphans; I will come to you." Jesus is speaking to his disciples. He is telling them that because he is their Almighty Father, they will never be orphaned. God will never leave them. I read the verse again while thinking of Mark, and I sense God saying to me that he will not leave Mark as an orphan. And not only is God offering himself as Mark's Almighty Father, it is also his intention to give Mark an earthly mother. I flip to the concordance at the back of my Bible to find other Scripture verses that will exonerate me from such a crazy idea. Instead I find a long list of verses that use the term "fatherless," including Hosea 14:3, which says, "...for in you the fatherless find compassion."

I am reminded of the prayer I prayed over and over when I was preparing for my trip to Uganda. *Break my heart for what breaks yours, God,* is what I asked. I know God has already answered this prayer; it is the only reason I have such a great burden for all the sick little babies under my care at the orphanage. *But adoption? Isn't that taking things a little far?*

It is good to be aware of the plight of the orphan and to be compassionate toward them. *But why ask me to get so involved? So hands-on? Can't I just feel this way from afar and support orphans another way? What if Mark doesn't live past this month?*

Besides, I'm too young, I plead to God later that evening. *I'm only twenty-two years old and I don't know anything about being a mother.* In the silence of the night, interrupted only by the occasional call of a cuckoo hawk outside my window, the Holy Spirit prompts me to turn to the book of First Timothy. The Apostle Paul wrote the following to Timothy to encourage him in his ministry to the church of Ephesus: "Don't let anyone look down on you because you are young, but set an example for the believers in speech, in conduct, in love, in faith and in purity" (1 Timothy 4:12).

This verse confronts my weak attempt to use age as a valid excuse to run from what God may be calling me to. Well, if God isn't going to accept that reason, I'll remind him that I am single. *What Mark needs is a family and I'm single. I can't do this on my own, God. Maybe if I were married this would seem reasonable. But I'm not married and I have no guarantee I will ever get married.*

You will not be doing this alone, God reassures me. He leads me to Isaiah:

See, the Sovereign LORD comes with power,
and he rules with a mighty arm.
See, his reward is with him,
and his recompense accompanies him.
He tends his flock like a shepherd:
He gathers the lambs in his arms
and carries them close to his heart;
he gently leads those that have young.
(Isaiah 40:10-11)

This last part strikes my soul. *He gently leads those that have young.* He is speaking about mothers. And he is reminding me that he gently leads them. *Okay, God,*

75

if those arguments don't stand up, what about the fact that I have no job here and am far away from my family who is my main support network? Also, I have absolutely no clue how to begin the adoption process or what it involves, and I have no desire to embark on such a daunting process alone. Again, in response God leads me to Isaiah:

> And if you spend yourselves in behalf
>   of the hungry
>   and satisfy the needs of the oppressed,
> then your light will rise in the darkness,
>   and your night will become like the noonday.
> The Lord will guide you always;
>   he will satisfy your needs in a sun-scorched land
>   and will strengthen your frame.
> You will be like a well-watered garden,
>   like a spring whose waters never fail.
> *(Isaiah 58:10-11)*

These words of truth serve to remind me that as a Christian I am to help the oppressed, for it is through such actions that God works to provide for and meet people's needs. God is not dependent on people to carry out his work; rather, he chooses to use us, knowing that in such service we will be drawn closer to him and experience contentment. Therefore, when one is in a position to help, it is only because God has orchestrated such a circumstance. "Freely you have received; freely give," Jesus tells his disciples (Matthew 10:8).

All that I have is ultimately God's, and the very fact that I am in a position to help Mark is because of God. God has blessed me with the family I have and the support they are to me, in part so that I may feel equipped by God to step out in faith. Jesus said, "From everyone who has been given much, much will be demanded; and from the one who has been entrusted with much, much more will be asked" (Luke 12:48b).

I take a deep breath and realize that for the first time today, I feel calm. Through his Scriptures, God has gently struck down excuse after excuse for why I am inadequate to respond in obedience to what he is asking of me, and the truths in these verses have flooded me with peace. God knows my thoughts, and he knew in advance the very excuses I would throw at him to persuade him to free me of his call. Rather than validate my excuses for why I am unequipped, God has shown me that I am perfectly equipped to carry out his calling because it is God himself who is going to bring it about. It is all about him, not me. It dawns on me why I feel such purpose when I am with Mark and why my heart is so broken for him. It is because God has been preparing me for this moment.

I close my Bible. I have never experienced anything like what has just happened. Never has God spoken to me in such an intimate way before, guiding me through his scriptures to help me understand his will for a particular situation. He truly is an all-knowing God. As I close my eyes, my head resting on my pillow, one last verse crosses my mind: "The only thing that counts is faith expressing itself through love" (Galatians 5:6b).

CHAPTER FIVE

December 2003, Uganda

B Y MONDAY evening I still have not uttered a word about this to anyone else other than Kirsten.

"I am so worried about all the kids, not just baby Mark," I share, confiding once again over the phone to my sister. "Their needs far exceed what the staff can give them." I wipe my eyes. *Why do I keep crying?* "I came here to help, and instead I feel so helpless, you know?"

"How are you feeling after the fast?" Kirsten asks. She hones in on the most important question, well aware that we never know how much time we have because of the unreliable connection.

"I believe that if I choose not to be obedient to God, I may regret it for the rest of my life. I think I will feel disconnected from God if I decide to disobey what I feel in my heart God is asking me to do. This is bigger than just me caring about Mark. I feel that my spirit, my soul, is inclined to adopt Mark not just because I love him and want him to live, but because God has shown me that this is a part of his greater plan."

Kirsten is quiet. She lets me speak and process my thoughts. How I wish I had my sister's wisdom. How I long for her to be here, to strengthen me with her faith.

"But if I do this, what does that mean for me? I will be a single mom. I don't want to be a single mom. I don't want to be a broke, young single mother. I don't want to take Mark away from his home and out of the country he was born in. I don't want to be looked at as the naïve young white girl who went to Uganda and brought home a little black baby. Because this is not what is going on. This desire did not come from me. God put it on my heart, and I just can't seem to shake the sense that it has to do with something that is bigger than me. Besides, I don't see how this is possible. My flight home is less than four months away, and there is no way that I am going to have anything legal in place by then. I don't even know where I am supposed to begin."

After a significant pause, Kirsten begins. "Tandy, I know you. I know that this is contrary to the plans you had when you went there. And you know what that says? That confirms to me that this is from God. I have been praying that God will harden your heart to this adoption if it is not his will, and that your heart will continue to be burdened by this and you will not feel released from it if it is his will. That you will go from fighting it to having a great sense of peace about it. The Bible is full of references about caring for orphans, Tand. James writes how those who care for widows and orphans in their distress are truly living out their faith. While I was praying for you, God kept giving me the same two verses over and over again from Psalm 68: 'A father to the fatherless, a defender of widows, is God in his holy dwelling. God sets the lonely in families.'

"God sets the lonely in families," she repeats. "And Tand," Kirsten continues, "we'll do this together, okay? All of your family here — we will all be Mark's family. We are all in this together. You are not alone in this. It won't be just you and Mark. Mark will be adopted by our whole family."

"I know. I know." I can feel the panic rising, so I try to take a deep breath. When I release it, a confession accompanies the warm air. "I'm just really scared. I believe that God can do the impossible. That is where some of my fear comes from. I'm scared that there is a very good chance that Mark will become my son. I am scared that the impossible will happen."

"Have you told Mom or Dad yet?" Kirsten asks gently.

"No. I will soon. I was just giving the whole situation some more time in case my feelings changed. I wanted to be sure that this decision was directed by God rather than based out of my own emotions. And I know how I feel for certain now and what I must do. I know."

To MY SURPRISE, Mom and Dad are rather calm when I give them the news that I am feeling a distinct call from the Lord to pursue adoption for Mark. Even though we share the same Christian faith, I have never used these words before with them — "called by God." Such words sound strange to me. But how else to say it? Our God is a relational, intimate God who speaks to all people in a variety of ways. I have been hearing his voice, and it is no longer possible for me to ignore it, try as I might.

"Tandy," my mom says to me, "I remember how nervous I was when you went off to Ghana with Volunteers for Peace. You were only seventeen and almost everyone else on the team was so much older than you. I didn't want to let you go, but your dad encouraged me not to hold you back. You know what your dad told me? He said, 'Laureen, we have made every effort to raise our children as global citizens, not just Canadian citizens.'

"We wanted you and Kirsten and Nathan to be aware of what was happening in other parts of the world," Mom continues. "Our faith in Christ is real, and this was how we felt called to live it out. To teach you that when you see a need, you are to step in and fill it rather than wait for someone else to help. I can't be hard on you for trying to do this, Tandy. Maybe God has been preparing you for this since you were a little girl. I don't know."

"Mom, do you remember a time when you felt you just had to do something even though you knew it was going to be really hard?" A brief silence hangs in the air, a sign Mom is deep in thought.

"Going to South Africa to work in the mission hospitals was hard," she replies. "It was really difficult to be there. In the face of so much suffering and death, as a physician you can only do so much. And many days, you just didn't feel that you were helping at all. That definitely was a faith-based decision for me. And if I had never gone there, I may not have married your dad." She takes a deep breath. "We are going to step up to the plate here, Tandy. This is up to you, and if you have been prayerful about this and it is really what you want, we will support you in that. We are behind you one hundred percent. No matter the cost, we will work it out."

I haven't yet brought up the issue that I have no idea how much the adoption will cost. I am pretty much broke. I have saved up just enough to cover my trip to Uganda. My plan had always been to live with Mom and Dad when I returned until I found a job and made enough money to get my own place.

"Being a mom is hard, Tandy. So hard. But I can't think of anything more valuable than providing a child with a family," Mom says with sincerity. "I love being a mom. I loved staying at home with you kids for those twelve years." She pauses. "There is something I never told you. I have always thought about adopting. I'm not sure if I lacked the courage or what, because I obviously never went through with it. Maybe this was a desire that was always meant to be fulfilled in the form of my first grandchild." Her voice sounds just as surprised as I feel.

Dad's response to my decision to begin the foster parent process is similar to Mom's.

"Tandy, I remember the first time in my life when I experienced something like what you are experiencing. While I was in South Africa, I felt a supernatural pull toward social justice. For the first time, I was seeing a tremendous amount of suffering and death from bad public policy, divided communities, and spiritually bankrupt individuals causing chaos. It was during this time that the connection between health, power, politics, money, employment, and employability was made excruciatingly clear to me. The significance of that experience cannot be overstated, for my life was dramatically changed from then on. What you are saying you need to do now, Tandy, with Mark—" I hear Dad take a deep breath. "I understand. I have no idea how it is going to happen but I understand."

I am astounded by the encouragement and affirmation that I have just received from my parents. Just as God has been preparing me for years for this, it looks like he has been preparing Mom and Dad's hearts as well.

I KNOW VERY little about the international adoption process. What I do know, I learned from my friends Peter and Mary-Anne, a couple I met during my first month in Mbale. They moved to Uganda from England for missions work seven years ago, and have since adopted two little girls from the children's home in Jinja where I am volunteering. It was, in fact, because of their connection to this orphanage that I chose to visit it in the first place. From my conversations with them, I've learned that the adoption process in Uganda starts by first getting approved as the child's foster parent. This would mean that Mark would no longer live at the orphanage, but would come home with me when my shift was over, sleep at my place, and then return with me and spend the day at the orphanage. For Peter and Mary-Anne, they had to foster their daughters for three years before they could apply for legal adoption rights.

I will never succeed in being approved as a foster parent if Margaret doesn't give a strong recommendation. The same day I speak with Mom and Dad, I ask Margaret if she has a couple of minutes for us to speak privately while Mark and the other children in my care have been put down for their afternoon nap. She brings me into her office and shuts the door.

"Are you all right?" she asks as we sit down.

Margaret leads the staff with a calm, no-nonsense demeanour. The housemothers respect her because her decisions are fair and firm. In all my time here, I have yet to see Margaret flustered. Her personality, combined with years of experience in this position, enables her to take everything in stride with a strong sense of assurance that she will figure out how to handle whatever surprises come her way. I take comfort in this character trait of hers, yet I am still a bit nervous about what I am going to share. So much weight hangs on her response. Will she be immediately supportive? What will she say? Margaret folds her long slim fingers together on her desk, patiently waiting for me explain why I have asked to speak alone with her.

"Yes, yes, I'm all right. Everything is fine," I reply. Then I quickly blurt out my reason for our talk before my nerves get the best of me. I share how my feelings for Mark have grown stronger ever since I was first overwhelmed with compassion for him the day he lay unresponsive on the mat.

"This longing for Mark initially caught me by great surprise," I tell her, "for adoption never crossed my mind when I made plans to come here." I describe how God has continued to affirm this decision and how I am now stepping out in faith that he is going to make this happen if it is his will.

Margaret tucks a stray strand of hair behind one ear. Her eyes are not unfriendly, yet I have never seen them look so serious. "You do realize," she asks me, "that Mark is the sickest of them all, Tandy? I have no hesitation supporting you in adopting one of the children here. But I do caution you with your decision. There are many healthy children here. Mark is so small; he'll never be strong."

"I know. I know he's really sick. But I'm not pursuing adoption because I've decided I want to be a mother. I'm pursuing it because I feel so strongly about Mark and the bond that I believe God has given us. It doesn't matter if he's healthy or not, weak or strong. All that matters is that it is Mark."

Margaret assures me that she will support me in every way she is able. She advises me to start the process immediately.

"You have very little time. It is now December, and you leave for Canada in March, right?" I feel the weight of urgency as I nod my head. She says I must begin right away by going to the Department of Probation and Social Welfare to pick up a foster parent application. She ushers me out of her office. "Go now," she whispers in my ear. She squeezes my hand briefly and nods toward the front door.

That evening as I rock Mark back and forth in my arms, waiting for him to drift off to sleep, I feel different. I am incredibly relieved with Margaret's reaction, and I seem to be experiencing a new-found sense of freedom after speaking with her. It is as though I can finally share a great and wonderful secret—I want to be Mark's mother. And even though nothing official has happened, I feel that I have crossed the first possible barrier and that the process is now underway.

Once Mark falls asleep, I sit down in the dining room with the application form. I am intimidated before my pen even makes contact with the paper.

The first heading reads, "The Republic of Uganda Foster Care Placements Prospective Foster Parent Record," and it demands I fill out my name, age, date of birth, district of origin, occupation, religion, marital status, and whether or not my marriage relationship is monogamous or polygamous.

Then I have to "State the income and wealth of the prospective Foster Parents" and "Give details of businesses and land owned by the family/person." What in the world am I going to write here that is going to give the officer any inkling that I can be trusted to provide for Mark financially?

The following section asks me to include "A description of the home." I write that the home is clean and safe with two bedrooms, a kitchen, a shower, and a toilet. It asks me to list the number of rooms (four) and the type of toilet (flushing). Wait. Did I read that right? Yes. It appears as though they are trying to judge a person's economic situation by their septic system.

Next I have to answer whether or not I need financial support to start fostering. "No support needed," I write. This is the truth. I have enough money for Mark and myself until I go home.

Then comes the most significant question of all: "Why does this family/person wish to foster children?" My pen pauses above the empty lines that follow. I don't want to make any mistakes here. Slowly and cautiously, I write, "I already love Mark as my own son and I wish to provide a loving home and a future for this particular child who does not have a family."

The next question asks, "Do they understand the temporary nature of fostering?" "I am fostering to adopt," I write. I finish by listing Margaret as my reference. I date each page Monday, December 8, 2003.

I have exactly three months to the day until I have to fly home.

WHEN I WRITE to friends back home about the situation and ask them to pray that I will be approved as Mark's foster parent, I get a variety of responses. Most are along the lines of "Wow, that's unbelievable" (also known as, "Wow, I don't know what to say. I can't relate to this on any level, so I'll try to say something neutral").

One friend in particular, a parent himself, cautions me with these words: "This isn't a puppy that you bring home, Tandela; this is a life." I know he feels a responsibility toward me, to help me think through my decision, but the words sting all the same. They also serve as a reminder that, to even my Christian friends who believe in faith-based decisions, I am still going to be "crazy Tandela" who traveled to Africa and tried to bring home a baby.

I try to explain to them that it is not so much that I want to adopt a child, but rather that I feel God is distinctively calling me to adopt Mark. Sometimes after such conversations I feel very alone. There are times when I feel that all I have to stand on are my own convictions, because no one else seems to be giving me many words of support. I know I shouldn't expect others to understand, for this is something personal God has laid on my heart and not theirs. But it's still hard.

I can use words like "I never planned for this" or "This is actually the opposite of what I had in mind when I went to Uganda" or "I just felt God leading me to do this," but no matter what I say, I know that I will be misunderstood by many as someone who just couldn't resist the cuteness of a certain baby, and who wanted to be a good person and play a saving role in a little boy's life.

When people respond by telling me, "Mark will never know how lucky he is that you are doing this for him" or "I could never do what you are doing, Tandy, you are a much better person than me," feelings of protection for Mark surface inside of me, and I long to shield him from being pitied and seen as the recipient of an act of charity.

"This is not about me wanting to be a good person!" I want to shout to the world. It is not being done out of the kindness of my heart. What is happening between me and Mark is a great deal more profound and difficult to articulate. It is as if God has gently reached down and placed his hand in front of the path that I was intending to take at this point in my life and is instead guiding me toward another that I never knew existed.

I MANAGE TO hand in the foster care application the day after my conversation with Margaret, and I hear back from the probation officer three days later. I am told that I have qualified for the second step in the foster care process and must now undergo a home study. This means the probation officer will come and inspect my rented quarters, ask me some questions, and assess whether these surroundings provide a fitting environment for a child.

The probation officer visits the following day and informs me that I will not qualify unless I buy more furniture. I am inclined to believe that this has more to do with him exercising his authority than anything else, but given he is the only probation officer in the region and possesses the power to deny me foster parent privileges at any point, I hold my tongue and refrain from arguing. I have him, Officer Nelson Makiywe, to thank for a small crib and an ugly secondhand couch, which together cost sixty thousand Ugandan shillings. The couch's three pillows look like they were used to shield bullets during the war that liberated Uganda from Idi Amin's dictatorship in 1979.

The next step in the home study is to introduce the probation officer to Mark. When he comes to the orphanage to meet Mark, Mr. Makiywe takes one look at him and says, "You should choose a fat baby."

I am used to such comments by now. The staff at the orphanage are aware of my intention to adopt Mark, and many have felt compelled to tell me that it would be wiser to choose a child with a greater chance of survival. This is a lot of trouble to go through if Mark is going to die soon, I am told. And though such comments seem harsh, I understand where they are coming from. There are many relatively healthy babies at the orphanage, ones that will undoubtedly survive their childhood, who are also greatly in need of a permanent home.

With the influx of so many comments about how weak Mark is and given my knowledge of the physician's prognosis, I can't help but contemplate the possibility that Mark is HIV-positive.

"With his dry skin, his weak immune system, and all those infections, he must have it," one of the housemothers remarked, speaking about HIV. "Mark looks the same as the other children here who have tested positive."

It is not uncommon for babies to be abandoned by

mothers who have been told they are HIV-positive. Such women, very sick themselves, believing that their newborns also have the virus, feel ill-equipped to tend to a weak and vulnerable child whose life will likely be short and full of suffering. *What other diseases or complications does Mark have,* I wonder. *There must be something that is causing all of his awful infections. In time, what long-term disabilities, diseases, or side effects will be uncovered because of the incredible malnutrition and suffering he experienced as a newborn?*

"I NOW MUST write you a letter saying you are a fit foster parent," Mr. Makiywe says, surveying my quarters for the second time. "That will cost six hundred thousand shillings."

I have to restrain myself from laughing with disbelief. This is ridiculous. It is Mr. Makiywe's job to write this letter, and by "write a letter" he is referring to signing my completed forms. What he is asking me to do is pay a bribe — a bribe equivalent to three hundred American dollars.

I have been warned that bribery goes hand in hand with adoption. Hopeful, expectant parents pay agencies a flat fee to help with international adoption logistics and have no idea that a portion of their money is going to bribe local authorities to stamp papers they should already be stamping. Everyone here knows that a family overseas committed to adoption will do almost anything to speed up the adoption process or ensure that it goes through. A few hundred dollars is nothing in comparison to being able to hold one's newly adopted child. But when it comes down to it, these corrupt practices mean that certain people are making money off of orphans. The children have become commodities. It makes me incredibly angry.

"I am not paying you a bribe, Mr. Makiywe." I silently pray to Jesus that he will intercede so that my refusal to participate in corrupt practices does not result in the denial of my foster request. Mr. Makiywe stiffens, looking taller than his six-foot stature. A vein protrudes slightly from his forehead as he clenches his jaw.

"I need a receipt for anything I pay you for," I continue. "If you write me a receipt for the letter, fine. But there is no way I am risking my adoption request by participating in anything illegal. If I am doing this, I have to make sure that every part is legitimate. So, I need a receipt for everything you ask me to pay you for."

Mr. Makiywe is silent for a time.

"I must leave now," he tells me. "I have many more

important things to take care of. I will have to think about this."

I CAN HARDLY believe it. Two days later, on Tuesday, December 16th, I am holding in my hands the first official document in my journey to adopt Mark. Mr. Makiywe has given me his signed approval, making me Mark's foster parent. And he ended up writing his "letter," a small paragraph that states:

> *Mark was abandoned at birth and brought to Mulago Hospital where he was then placed in a children's home. Tandela stays in a permanent home within a good compound. She works as a volunteer with the children's home where Mark has been living and is very willing to provide full custody to Mark.*

The day after I receive these papers, I bring Mark home with me. I have arranged with Margaret to take two weeks off so that I can fully devote myself to Mark and help him defy the physician's recent prognosis that he will not survive the next month. There is no guarantee that we have much time left together, and I want to spend every minute of it with him. I am determined to do everything I can to bond with him and make up for some of the maternal neglect that Mark has suffered since his birth.

I don't know if anything in the world could have prepared me for what the next two weeks had in store.

CHAPTER SIX

December 2003–January 2004, Uganda

H IS WAIL pierces my ears. Every fierce cry makes his little body shake. His lips, massively swollen due to illness, are out of place on his tiny face. I rock him back and forth in my room while my limbs groan with exhaustion. I seldom put him down because I can't bear to let him writhe hysterically on the bed. He is too sick. His eyes wander around the room as he looks everywhere but at me. His screams are so loud and constant I wonder if the owners of my servants' quarters think I am abusing him.

I hold Mark in my arms, giving him what no medication can: my touch and my love. And yet, after ten days of constant attention, he offers no sign of recognition, no evidence that I'm anything more than a stranger. Not once have his eyes flickered with the faint acknowledgment that it is my voice that has been singing softly to him every day and praying for God to spare his life.

Fight, Mark, fight. I love you.

A tear slides down my cheek, already dampened by the inescapable humidity of Jinja. This is not how it was supposed to be. This was supposed to be time we really bonded with one another, when Mark would begin to identify me as someone more than a housemother. I thought that our days would be full of cuddles and getting to know each other outside the orphanage walls. I had hoped that after a few days of one-on-one time, Mark would not only acknowledge my presence but would begin to grow attached to me. I thought his health was going to improve, not get worse.

I must now come to terms that what Mark needs to survive extends far beyond what I or any physician can offer. He needs a miracle.

OUR TIME ALONE, our chance to bond, is almost at an end. My days have been full of exhaustion, sweat, and doubt, and the many tears that have been shed haven't just been Mark's. Who was I kidding, thinking I could do this on my own? Maybe I didn't really hear God at all. I'm definitely not equipped for this. Mark needs someone who knows what they are doing. Not me. Not a twenty-two-year-old with no experience. Mark won't even look at me. Is it because I am doing something wrong? Is it because he isn't going to survive?

Why would you ask me to do something this hard, God? It is day thirteen of the fourteen days Margaret has allowed me to take leave from the orphanage. After tomorrow, this will still be Mark's home, but during the day he will have to share me with the rest of the children at the orphanage.

My tears of frustration cool slightly against my cheeks as a breeze rolls by, a contrast to the noonday sun beating down on me as I wash a bunch of Mark's dirty cloth diapers outside. *Why won't Mark stop crying? Why does he look everywhere but at me? Doesn't he know I love him? Doesn't he know I would do anything for him, that I long to understand the source of his cries?* My fatigued arms wring out the diapers, and I hastily hang them to dry. Mark will wake up from his nap any minute now.

As I drape the diapers over the clothesline, my mind wanders to Isaiah 58:11, one of the instrumental verses God used to communicate his calling for me to adopt Mark. The verse says:

> The LORD will guide you always;
>> he will satisfy your needs in a sun-scorched land
>> and will strengthen your frame.
> You will be like a well-watered garden,
>> like a spring whose waters never fail.

I feel like anything but a well-watered garden in a sun-scorched land! I feel like a dried-up stream full of sticks and mud, devoid of life. These past two weeks have worn me out. It is only by God's grace that I can continue to care for Mark. Each day when I have nothing left to give, God has reached down into the reserves of my soul and supplied me with strength. Yet I see no answer to my prayers for Mark, no sign that his health is getting any better.

I hear him whimper from inside and I rush in, grabbing his bottle from the kitchen counter on the way.

"Hi, Mark. I'm here. It's okay, sweetie," I reassure him as I bend down and pick him up out of the crib. His eyes are shut as he moves his head from side to side. He opens and closes his mouth a little, a sign that gives me hope he may swallow some formula. I bought it for him, knowing it's a much healthier alternative to the porridge served at the orphanage. I nudge his chin upward to insert the newborn-sized nipple into his tiny mouth and whisper to him as he begins to drink.

From deep within me, I continue to ache for Mark. Though the last two weeks have been very trying, my maternal feelings for Mark have only grown. As a child is woven in his mother's womb, God has woven in my heart a longing to tend to Mark as devotedly as a mother tends to her newborn child. When he is sleeping, I gaze at him in wonder. This is when he looks most at peace. Long, dark eyelashes drape over his eyes, and his chest rises and falls with each soft rhythmic breath. I am in awe that God has allowed me to care for such a beautiful little child.

I stare at Mark's hands, folded in little fists, and have a hard time believing that I was once the same size. That in fact everyone begins as a tiny, helpless baby, dependent on others to give them what they need to live. For many of us, those people who care for us as infants are our birth parents. Whether they want to or not, they are responsible for providing for us day after day. When I look at Mark, I feel no obligation to help him. It is the opposite. I *want* to be the one who provides for his needs. I *want* to be the most important person in his life. As each day passes, my longing to officially be his mother grows.

"Do you know me?" I whisper softly, my voice barely audible against Mark's rhythmic sucking of the bottle. "Who am I to you?"

I am almost crushed by the sudden weight of my sobs, fearing that Mark is on his way out of this broken world. Only God knows if what I am doing is nurturing Mark back to life or offering him palliative care. I long for someone to hold me and reassure me that everything is going to be okay.

I squeeze my eyes shut to stop my tears. My arms are both occupied, one wrapped securely around Mark while the other supports his bottle. I take a deep breath as the last tears slide down my cheeks, remoistening my already damp shirt. I keep my eyes closed. I know all too well the dreary view that will greet my gaze, for I have been confined to these grey walls nearly twenty-four hours a day for almost two weeks. Mark's body quivers, working hard with each suck and swallow. As he finishes the last of the formula, his sucks become light and shallow. Then they stop. I slowly open my eyes and lean forward to see if he has fallen asleep.

His body is still. He rests one hand in the other. He looks peaceful. Then, I notice his eyes. They are wide open and they are fixated on something.

Me.

For the first time in the eight weeks that I have known him, Mark's eyes meet my own. His small black pupils are still, focusing on mine. Excitement shoots through me as I comprehend the significance of this moment. In a split second, all of my doubts and insecurities over how Mark feels about me are driven away, all because of what Mark is saying to me as he stares at my face. He knows I am here. And he knows that I am never going to desert him.

AFTER MARK MAKES eye contact with me, he begins to consistently eat yogurt and mashed banana, and the vomiting and diarrhea are instantly almost non-existent. A few days after finally settling into a routine and returning to day shifts at the orphanage, Mark sits up by himself for the first time. I am feeling more and more optimistic about his chances of survival.

It is now the beginning of January, and all the government offices will re-open this week following their Christmas holiday closure. Now that Mark is officially my foster child, I can start on the paperwork necessary for him to accompany me home in March. Since I'm not sure where exactly to begin, I decide to call my friends in Mbale, Peter and Mary-Anne, the British couple who have twice successfully pursued international adoption here in Uganda. While I haven't heard all the details regarding their two adoption journeys, it seems like both times the process was fraught with great frustration. It wouldn't surprise me if they weren't optimistic about my plan to adopt Mark.

Peter answers the phone. I ask him how he, Mary-Anne, and their two girls are doing, and then I fill him on what I've been up to in Jinja. Finally, I tell him about Mark, and my decision to begin the process of adoption.

"Can you give me some advice on what I need to do to get paperwork for Mark to get into Canada?" I ask.

"Tandela, you need to be realistic," Peter cautions me. "It is going to take years to get that kind of documentation in order."

"But what do I have to do to begin? I've got just over two months. Surely I can make something happen in two months."

"Tandela, I have to be honest. You wouldn't believe how difficult and time-consuming it has been for Mary-Anne and me to get the information we needed from the Ugandan authorities to take our girls home to England for a temporary visit. I can't put into words how emotionally draining this has been for us. You have to prepare yourself that this is probably not going to happen for you."

"But I can work quickly."

"Tandela, it is impossible to get a visa for Mark in two months' time. The birth certificate, the passport, the visa — this is all paperwork that has taken us six years to get. *Six years*. What makes you think that your situation with Mark is going to be any different? If anything, it will take longer because you are young and single. The odds are not in your favour."

I pause. I don't need Peter to tell me that I am entirely unequipped to begin the complicated adoption process. This I know.

But it's not as though this was ever my idea in the first place.

I want to respond by saying, "I realize that it happened that way for your family; however, I think this is being orchestrated by God," but I keep my mouth shut. Such words will come across as incredibly arrogant and insensitive. *Time will tell if this is meant to happen*, I say to myself. And it will only happen if God does something miraculous. Because there is no other way. This situation necessitates the performance of a miracle. Or two or three.

"Can you at least tell me how I would *begin* the process?" I press Peter.

"Okay. You can only apply for adoption after you've fostered the child for three years, though in the meantime the authorities may be willing to grant Mark a temporary visa to Canada so that you can visit your family. In order to get this visa for Mark, he must first have a valid passport, and in order to get a passport, he needs a birth certificate."

Birth certificate. Right. Of course it all begins with a birth certificate. But abandoned babies left in latrines do not come with paperwork. How do you get a birth certificate for someone who, on paper, does not exist?

"THIS IS ALL that we have regarding Mark's birth." Margaret's brow furrows as she skims over a piece of paper she has just retrieved from a filing cabinet in her office. "I wish there was more we could offer you." She hands me the paper, allowing me to read the contents firsthand.

The paper is a short report from the hospital regarding Mark's admittance after he was discovered in the latrine. All that it says is that he was found in the district of Makindye outside of Kampala on March 11th, 2003, and taken to the Mulago Hospital, where he was named Abandoned Mark.

"That is pretty much all that we know about where he came from. And I don't think it is official enough to get a birth certificate authorized. But the police station in Makindye may have kept a record of him being discovered. It was, after all, a police officer who delivered Mark to the hospital. Maybe they wrote up a report that proves Mark has no known relatives."

"And if the police station doesn't have anything?" I ask.

"I don't know. The best-case scenario is that the process will just take a lot longer." Margaret pauses. I can see her wrestle with the words that she obviously feels she must say. Finally, she stretches out her arm and rests her hand on my shoulder. "No part of me wants this, but I must tell you the truth: the worst-case scenario is the process will be stalled for years, and perhaps forever. The authorities will encourage you to instead choose a child with a simpler case who has existing documentation demonstrating they are indeed an orphan with no known family members who can be located."

Margaret says there is no point in worrying about

that until I have gone to Makindye and paid the police station a visit. "You must go to Makindye soon," she urges me, "and then you can decide what to do from there."

It is a challenge for me to focus on dinner that evening. I am distracted by my thoughts of Makindye and what I may or may not find when I go there. Mark is in a particularly good mood this evening. He plays with me as I feed him a mixture of rice and beans, swooping his head in for each bite and smiling victoriously with each mouthful. Two little teeth are budding out of his upper gums. I'm thankful that the teething hasn't seemed to bother him.

I hurry up and down the row of children, spooning food into the babies' mouths. Even though Mark obviously favours me, he doesn't seem to get jealous when he has to share me during the day with the other children in my care. I don't know if this is because he is still growing in his attachment to me or if it is a reflection of his easygoing personality. *Will Mark be in my life long enough for me to learn this?* It is hard to believe that the beginning of this answer lies within a little town outside of Kampala.

Sharon walks home with me and Mark after dinner, and after Mark falls asleep, we sit down for a cup of tea. She has been away visiting her sister in Kampala for most of the Christmas holidays, and it has been a while since we have been able to talk one-on-one. I fill her in on what I learned in Margaret's office and my plan to visit Makindye as soon as possible.

"I can't believe how well Mark is doing," Sharon joyfully remarks. She marvels at how his strength has improved and how he loves to laugh and play on the mats with the other babies. "And the way that he looks at you," Sharon shakes her head, smiling. "His little face just lights up when you walk into a room."

Sharon tells me that she has been praying for us, specifically that our bond would continue to grow.

"I'm sure you know that Mark cares for you," she shares, her eyes glowing reassuringly. "But I want you to know that everyone else sees it, too. Mark has changed dramatically ever since you began fostering him. He has come alive."

Her words seep into my heart, relaxing the tightly wound fibres of doubt and anxiety.

"My school doesn't begin for another week and a half," Sharon continues, "so I am free to go with you to Makindye, if you'd like."

I ask her how soon she can go. Today is Tuesday, January 6th, and I am hoping to go within the next few days.

She lifts her cup to her lips, her beautiful dark eyes a shining contrast to the white mug.

"How about tomorrow?"

SHARON AND I arrive at Jinja's taxi park at eight o'clock the next morning. I hurriedly swallow the last of a granola bar. Busy with getting Mark settled at the orphanage this morning, I hadn't had time to eat breakfast. White matatus* are parked in disarray across the dirt field. The vans comfortably seat about sixteen people, but I usually see twice as many bodies crammed within the cabs. We look for a matatu that indicates it is headed to Kampala by looking at the signs on the roofs. Sharon spots one and walks up to the driver. She says something to him in Swahili. He points toward another matatu nearby.

"Over here, Tandela," she calls. "This is the next taxi to Kampala. We will have to wait until there are enough passengers for it to leave." We climb into the matatu and pay the driver our fare of three thousand shillings.

Twenty minutes later, we depart the taxi park and take a left turn, making our way toward Kampala Road, which then will lead us to the highway. I rest my elbows on the windowsill and begin to take in the

---

* Matatu: Taxi van.

sights. Air wafts in as we pick up speed, softening the pungent smell of body odour inside the taxi. We pass the Jinja Training School for Nursing and Midwifery. Soon after, a large billboard advertising Nile Special Beer looms over us declaring it "Consistent. Trusted. Admired."

We drive across a bridge where the massive Lake Victoria flows into the Nile River. The distant shoreline is spotted with red clay roofs peeking out among leafy green bushes. I catch a glimpse of a crocodile floating motionless in the water below, the top half of its body exposed to the morning sun. On our side of the lake, telephone lines run juxtaposed above a cluster of straw huts along the water's edge. We fall into line behind a pickup truck loaded with bags of charcoal for cooking. The bags are stacked over five feet above the cab, and on top of them sit four men, their body weight holding the bags down. They rest their arms on their knees as they gaze at the view before them. Not long after we enter a town called Nakibizi, the pickup truck is suddenly pulled over by traffic police.

"Too many men sitting in the back of the truck," Sharon explains, smiling at the puzzled expression on my face. "Now the police will either give them a ticket or demand a bribe."

Our matatu manoeuvres around the situation, slowing down only slightly as it passes the police motorcycle, and continues on through the town. We make a brief stop to pick up three more passengers, even though we are well over capacity. Perhaps the traffic police are less concerned with overcrowded matatus than personal vehicles. Our driver has done a decent job of weaving us through the constant traffic on the highway, but I for one would feel a lot more secure if the taxi were equipped with seat belts. Getting in a car crash and being sent to the hospital is the last thing I need.

Outside a bright green building, what appears to have once been a store but is now a multi-family home, sits a young woman. Her hair is short and she wears no makeup. Her eyelids sag, and she looks as though she could fall asleep any minute. A baby grips the v-neck of her pink and green floral dress and pulls it toward him as he nurses, slightly exposing her breast. I am mindful of staring and turn away.

As we near the edge of the town we pick up speed and the sights begin to whip by. Once we are back on the highway, we drive alongside hand-harvested sugar plantations and the seemingly unending rolling hills of bright green tea plantations, both of which provide a beautiful backdrop. Never in my life have I experienced such lush surroundings. For a minute the highway clears of oncoming traffic and I can hear the gentle chirp of the small grey Nigrita birds as we enter the magnificent Mabira Forest.

"It is seventy-four thousand acres," Sharon gently interrupts my daydreaming. "But the newspapers say that in time part of it will be turned into sugar plantations. Look! A red-tailed monkey."

The forest is full of monkeys. At one time the forest also boasted lions, big antelope, and numerous hyenas. Beams of sunlight dance upon thousands of shimmering leaves that adorn trees in various brilliant shades of green. The sharp scent of pine cuts through the air. One can't help but feel a sudden rush of peace within such serene surroundings.

Once outside the forest, we drive through Lugazi, home of a large sugar factory. On our left we see labourers pick a tea plantation by hand. A sign for defensive driving looms over the roadway: "Do not play chicken with trucks or buses."

As we get closer to Kampala, the air grows strong with the smell of smoke from thousands of people cooking over outdoor charcoal fires. Rows of rickety shacks made from wood and clay lean against one another, as though if one were to fall they would all collapse like dominoes. Some of the shacks function as storefronts while others are homes.

The road becomes increasingly congested as more boda-bodas* and bicycles mix in with cars and trucks as we near Kampala. A diesel truck approaches in the on-coming lane, making me quickly reach for the window lever. It wobbles and threatens to come off in my hand. Just as the cracked rubber seal meets the frame, black smoke obscures my view. Sharon's low laugh is almost lost in the passing engine's roar.

"There is the Mandela National Stadium," Sharon points out the newly reopened window. "It is the home of our national football team, the Uganda Cranes." The stadium looks out of place, surrounded by acres of greenery with a few well-built homes dispersed throughout.

"And up there, on that hill to your left, is the house of the king of the Central Region."

We suddenly lurch forward in our seats as the taxi brakes to avoid hitting a pedestrian. I thrust my arms toward the seat in front of me, hoping to spare my neck from absorbing the impact. The air is polluted with the sounds of car horns, large trucks slamming on their

---

* *Boda-boda: Motorcycle taxi.*

brakes, and motorcycles revving their engines. I glance out a window across the aisle. Atop a mound of trash, the biggest stork I have ever seen fills its massive beak with garbage. The bird's wings are black and its long legs look like they are stained with excrement.

We slowly regain speed as we enter Kampala. Where roads converge, traffic directors dressed in white uniforms, black boots, and berets try to maintain order. From the architecture of the homes it becomes increasingly clear Kampala experiences a greater discrepancy between the rich and the poor. Rarely in Jinja did I encounter people begging, but already I have seen numerous people pleading for spare change.

When we arrive at the taxi park in Kampala, the scene is chaotic. There must be over a hundred matatus alone parked here, and the crowds of people and randomly scattered kiosks make it difficult to find a direct path anywhere. Sharon takes my hand and weaves us through, finding a matatu that will take us to Makindye. It is a short ride, only about fifteen minutes. When the taxi stops to let us out, Sharon asks the driver in Luganda where the police station is. He points to his right and tells her it is about a ten-minute walk.

The police station looks nothing like I expected. Instead of a distinguished building whose exterior imparts the order and authority of the law, most of the station is outdoors, consisting of an open court-yard surrounded by a perimeter of holding cells with an office in one corner. Voices holler in our direction. The crude sounds escaping from the cells grow louder, quickening our steps. Cheeks red with the sudden attention, Sharon and I keep our eyes fixed on the office ahead, refusing to acknowledge the jeers.

The officer at the front desk asks how he can help me, and I explain that I am looking for a police report on a particular abandoned baby.

"Mmm-hmm," he says, leafing through some papers in from of him. "And why do you need this paper?"

"I am planning on adopting him," I reply, "and I need this report in order to have a birth certificate processed." The officer removes his glasses and carefully, slowly, lays them on the desk.

"You are saying this baby was abandoned," he states.

"Yes," I confirm.

"And you are trying to adopt him? You? Are you even older than twenty?" I direct my gaze at the thin gold chain around his neck, respectfully averting his stare. He fixates on my face with suspicious eyes, as though trying to gauge how much inconvenience this request will cause him.

"Mark was found on March 11th, 2003, so that should be the date of the report. If you could take a look for me I would really appreciate it." I force myself to speak in a higher voice than usual, with a phony cheerfulness used only for the most desperate of favours.

"There is a good chance that this paper has not been preserved," he informs me. "Why would we need it? Who is going to come looking for the documentation of an abandoned baby? I don't even know where we file such things." He lifts and lowers his shoulders in a nonchalant shrug, casually dismissing the significance of this precious paper as though it were no more than an outdated parking ticket. "But I'll take a look. Have a seat outside."

Sharon and I walk out past the rusty door to the courtyard. We sit down on some stones meant to function as chairs. The air, devoid of any breeze, is intense with the powerful scent of body odour and urine-stained clothing. The men, crammed into the surrounding cells like chickens, look like they have been there for days and are covered in filth. For once I am glad that I do not understand Luganda or Swahili. I exchange sympathetic glances with Sharon.

We sit on the uncomfortable stones in the sweltering heat for four hours. I try to distract myself by thinking of Mark. He will be outside now, likely having spent most of his time sitting on a mat, fascinated with watching the older children play. When Mark is awake, he is constantly observing the activity around him. Rather than be the centre of attention, Mark seems very content to just observe the action and chaos around him. I always wonder what he thinks about as he takes it all in.

At the sound of the squeaking hinge, my eyes snap open.

"Miss Swann?" the officer beckons me inside. I hurry in, anxious to take a copy of the report to the registrar's office to get a birth certificate made. As of today I have less than eight weeks to accomplish everything.

"We cannot find it. I am sorry, we do not know where it is or if we have that record here," the desk sergeant tells me. *No, no, no!* My heart surges with adrenaline. Time is running out. If I do not get this report, I have nothing concrete to use to apply for Mark's birth certificate. My discouragement is compounded by my belief that, despite his initial reassurance, the officer has not spent the last four hours looking for the report.

"What am I supposed to do?" I utter a panicked whisper in Sharon's direction. "I don't have any other options."

"Can you look again?" Sharon pleads with the officer.

"I have already spent enough of my day looking for it," he snaps. His lips purse and with firm resolve he crosses his muscular forearms against his chest. "I'm sorry, I cannot do anything more." He turns away, occupying himself with another task.

We walk back outside, despondent. I raise my face upward, searching the clouds for answers. *What do you want me to do now, God? Why couldn't you just produce that report?*

"John!" Sharon cries out, inclining my attention toward a young policeman just entering the compound.

"Sharon, how are you? What a surprise!" John stretches out his hand as he greets her. He is tall, with lanky limbs and a shaved head. His demeanour is warm, as is his smile. He nods in acknowledgment as Sharon introduces us. "John and I were at the same school until he graduated a few years ago," she explains.

"What brings you here? Are you in trouble?" His smile fades and the crinkles beside his eyes disappear as his lips draw tight with concern.

"Tandela and I are here because we need a report documenting the discovery of a baby who was found in a pit latrine. Tandela wants to adopt the baby and needs this for the rest of his documentation."

John softly bites his lower lip, deep in thought.

"Do you know the date he was found?" he asks.

"The hospital told the orphanage that he was brought in on March 11th, 2003, so we think that is probably the day." Sharon's voice sounds suddenly hopeful.

"I will take a look for you."

I close my eyes, deeply exhaling with relief, and John adds with a smile, "It would be my pleasure."

I sit back down on the stone and rest my elbows on my knees, lowering my head into my hands. Sharon puts her hand on my back.

"It is going to be okay, Tandela," she tries to reassure me. I close my eyes and pray the report will be found this time. This is so much more stressful than I anticipated. I am beginning to get a glimpse of what Peter meant when he warned me that pursing adoption would be more difficult and time-consuming than I could imagine.

"If every step in the journey is going to be this challenging, I don't know if I can do this," I whisper to Sharon. It is now past four o'clock, meaning we will not be visiting the registrar's office today. The compound has little shade to offer, so I doubt my fair skin has been spared a sunburn. Sharon and I have eaten the other two granola bars that I brought with me, and my bottle of water is almost empty. Other than John and a small flock of pigeons, no one else has come into the courtyard all afternoon.

"You will not believe this — I found it!" John rushes out of the office, very pleased with himself. "I cannot believe it," he confesses. "I cannot believe I managed to recover this single paper among all the files in the office. It wasn't even where it should have been. Nothing is where it should be," he adds, disgruntled. The paper is blank but for the following: "Baby boy found in the bottom of a pit latrine on March 11, 2003." Underneath is scrawled "Immaculate."

"What does this mean?" I ask John, pointing at the word.

"Yes, I had that same question. I asked about it inside, and they told me that it is the name of the woman who was questioned when this case was investigated. We try to learn who the mother is in all of these kinds of cases." John gives me a rare direct gaze, searching my eyes. "But this woman was released, so she must have said she had nothing to do with the birth."

THE AIR OUTSIDE the compound is refreshingly sweet, devoid of the assaulting scent of sweat and urine radiating from the cells. We wearily trace our steps back to the taxi park. Sharon finds us a taxi that will take us directly to our hostel. It is nearly seven o'clock when we check in at the Red Chilli Hideaway. There are four wicker chairs stationed around a coffee table in the hostel's common room, and I lower myself into one, slouching forward with fatigue. A television roars in the background as two young Englishmen play pool and watch a soccer game. The walls are painted brick red and decorated with stencils of brown fish and lizards.

The suspense at the police station was almost too much. The sounds around me vaguely fade into the background and my vision becomes blurry as the last of the adrenaline subsides. I force myself to blink, bringing everything into sharper focus. It is no surprise my body is fading, for I have barely eaten today.

"Sharon?" She is sitting at one of the two communal computers, checking her email. "Can I get you something for dinner?"

"What are you going to have, Tandela?" she asks, absorbed in her typing.

"A pizza, I think." Out of all the international foods on the wall-mounted menu, pizza is the most comforting.

"I'll have the same, thank you." She logs off and turns around. She examines my wearied face, concern in her eyes. "Are you okay?" Once again I am aware of how Sharon is so much more mature than her sixteen years.

"Yeah, I'm fine." I get up to order, but suddenly I feel compelled to share how grateful I am that she is here. "Sharon? Thanks for coming with me. It means so much. And today… well, if you weren't here I wouldn't have got the report. And maybe I would have to say goodbye to Mark and —"

"Tandela," she cuts me off, "you would have found a way. God would have provided a way. Don't think about that. I'm glad I could help. We got the report! Don't look so sad," she jests. "I feel like we are on some top secret investigation," she whispers, her eyes twinkling.

While the pizzas are being prepared, I wander outside. The evening air is soothing after a long day of travel and sitting under the hot sun. My white flip-flops are now almost the same shade as the red dirt beneath my feet. Various tropical plants and trees displaying bright red and pink flowers surround the property, and the refreshing smell of spearmint fills the air.

The children will be getting their baths right now before they go to bed. I hope Mark will be okay without me tucking him in tonight. I miss him. I think of him sleeping and how utterly serene and peaceful he looks when he is curled up on his side with his mouth slightly gaping, his arms clasped around his little teddy bear.

I am still in shock that I actually have the one paper in the whole world that officially documents Mark's birth, the only concrete evidence that he is indeed an orphan. I have placed it between the pages of my Bible, which I keep with me in my purse. This paper is the most precious treasure I have ever had in my possession. I need to photocopy it and get a proper folder for it. After being approved as a foster parent, this is the second door that has opened for me on the journey toward adoption.

On the way to Makindye, I told myself if I did all that I physically could to secure information on Mark that could be used to generate a birth certificate and was forced to come away empty-handed, I would take that as a sign that this was probably not meant to be. I tried to prepare myself for the possibility that not getting any further in the adoption process could be part of God's plan. Perhaps the personal journey that had to take place in my heart — the willingness to step out in faith — was itself the reason for this whole experience. Could it be that the spiritual growth borne out of my surrendering my plans for my life and submitting to God's will was the real purpose?

Yet the door was not closed today. And now with the first mountain moved I am both excited and frightened. It was as I said to Kirsten: My trepidation comes not from believing the adoption is impossible, but rather believing that God will do the impossible if it is his plan. And the result is that I will be a mother, and not only that, but a single mother. And I feel very unprepared and ill-equipped to be anyone's mother at the moment.

I love Mark with all my heart, yet I am still uncomfortable with the possibility that my life may soon permanently change. Depending on how the next two months go, I am either going to be able to bring Mark home with me to Canada temporarily, possibly having to return back here after only six months, or I will have to extend my time in Uganda. Either situation makes it unlikely that I can apply for graduate school. Will I have to give up that dream for good? From this point in time onward, will I have to put all my needs and wants behind Mark's? I'm not ready for this, for the permanency of parenthood.

I sit down at the foot of an old acacia tree. Its base is wrapped in hundreds of roots that reach up its trunk and toward the sky. Once a little seedling, this tree is now the grandfather from which hundreds of younger heirs draw their life. Leaning against it, my anxiety begins to dissipate. This tree reminds me that we grow into who we need to be, by God's grace.

God, I want nothing to do with this if it is not of your will, I pray. *Harden my heart toward Mark and remove any desire to adopt him. Intercede so that tomorrow this will all stop if this is not of you. But if it* is *your will, you need to carry me, Jesus. Because this is really difficult. I am really scared. Continue to give Mark eyes that show me he loves me. I need that. I need confirmation from him that he cares for me too.*

I take a deep breath, appreciating the invigorating aroma of the surrounding foliage. I am reminded of the words that God spoke to the Apostle Paul when Paul was suffering: "My grace is sufficient for you, for my power is made perfect in weakness" (2 Corinthians 12:9). *You are right in thinking you are weak, my child,* I sense God whispering to me. *You are not supposed to feel strong. I am the strong one.*

CHAPTER SEVEN

January–February 2004, Uganda

THE NEXT morning, I am the first one awake in our dorm. I get dressed quietly, then gently shake Sharon awake. Once downstairs, we each have a bowl of oatmeal, then I check us out of the hostel and arrange for a taxi pick-up.

"I think I know where it is from here," Sharon says as we get out of the taxi in the heart of downtown Kampala. She is referring to the Ministry of Constitutional Affairs, the office that hopefully will process Mark's birth certificate. We search for the building on foot for twenty minutes.

"The problem is sometimes they move the ministries around and change the offices," Sharon explains apologetically. She asks for directions from a traffic director who then solicits advice from a nearby boda-boda driver.

We walk two blocks east and find ourselves facing the National Theatre building. Up ahead on our left looms a tall office building, painted white but faded with time. The building is commonplace for Kampala, consisting of barred windows and a heavy wrought-iron gate. A leafy tree protrudes from the sidewalk, shading a newspaper stand. Two women sit on the ground, their backs against the gate. One is braiding the other's hair. Trees and shrubs have been strategically planted around the property for privacy. Guards are stationed at various entry points. Above one of the entrances, a sign reads, "SILENT court in progress." The Ugandan national flag waves high above the building, and just below is the sign we have been searching for: Ministry of Justice and Constitutional Affairs Headquarters.

As soon as we take two steps inside, we are instructed to hand over our purses and walk through security. A sign above the security entrance says, "Abandon Firearms." Hands rummage through my belongings, and I nervously wonder what past events have transpired within these walls to cause such formal security procedures.

"Can you please direct me to where I go to get a birth certificate?" I ask the guard who hands me back my purse. He points down the hall in front of him then turns away. At the first right we see a woman sitting in a booth behind a sheet of glass. The booth reminds me of a ticket window at a movie theatre.

"I need to have a birth certificate made for my foster child," I explain to her. She hands me a form and a pen, then gestures us to a row of seats down the hall. Even though we arrived shortly after the opening time, we are not the only ones here. I am, however, the only white person. We take a seat, and I stare at the form. It asks me to fill in Mark's first name, middle name, and last name.

I have been praying about what Mark's middle name should be, anticipating that when I filled out the form for his birth certificate it would be required. I want to give Mark a middle name that reflects his Ugandan heritage and has a special meaning. Sharon and I talked about this back in Jinja, and she provided a number of names to consider that had their roots in different Ugandan dialects. And now, as I stare at the form, I know without a doubt the name I will choose:

Kirab, short for Kirabo, which means "gift" in Luganda. This is what Mark is to me, a gift from God.

I fill in "Mark Kirab."

I pause before writing his last name. Mark doesn't have an official family name. The very term "family name" assumes that a person is part of a family. I tap the paper with my pen. *Lord, what am I supposed to do here?* The pen seems to write itself as the word "Swann" scrawls across the paper. My last name. Our last name. As Mark's foster parent, I am the closest thing he has to a family. I raise my eyes toward the ceiling as they start to water, holding back my tears. I blink repeatedly in an effort to fight off this sudden rush of emotion.

Mark Kirab Swann. It feels a bit surreal.

The next line asks me for his date of birth. For most people, this would be a straightforward question. However, no one knows the exact day that Mark was born. I know only the date that he was discovered, March 11th, 2003. From examining the insects and other debris that had settled on his tiny three-pound body while in the latrine, along with the dire state of his health, doctors estimated he had been born maybe one or two days before he was found. I decide that the day two arms reached down and rescued Mark, bringing him out of a hole of darkness and into the light, would be his official birthday.

March 11th, 2003. The day the rest of his life began. I hand the completed form back to the clerk.

"Thank you. Please have a seat while I type up the certificate. I'll need you to look over it and verify that the information is correct," the woman informs me. After an hour in a sticky, hard chair, the clerk calls me back up.

The certificate is a legal-size piece of paper, and includes not only Mark's name and date of birth but also the information from the police report about him being abandoned in a pit latrine. Under the column for mother's name the woman has typed "Unknown." The father's name is also listed as "Unknown." Beside this is a column in which the ministry is required to write the name of the authority figure that attests to the truthfulness of this information.

"Mukedi, Robert, Divisional Crime Officer who discovered the child," the woman has typed. It is bizarre to look at a birth certificate for a little boy who has been "discovered" and whose parents share the name "Unknown." By God's grace maybe one day Mark will have a new birth certificate with my name on it.

"Everything looks good," I say, handing it back.

"Once this is authorized, we will mail it to you," the clerk says, inserting the file in an overflowing stack of papers.

"But I need it today. Can I get it signed today?"

"We don't usually do that," she replies, her eyes widening in surprise. "This certificate has to be authorized by the registrar general herself, you see. I just hand them off to my boss at the end of the day and she sees to it that the certificates get signed. We can't be bothering the registrar general every time a certificate needs her signature or she'd never get to much more important matters."

Before my very eyes, the form has vanished into a disheveled pile of paperwork. After my experience at the police station, I am not willing to let this form get misplaced, nor do I have the time to wait for it to be processed. Every step that lies ahead depends on having this paper in hand. I must make the clerk sympathetic to my cause.

"I completely understand," I begin, "it's just that I'm waiting for a passport so that my foster son can come with me to visit my family. But the passport application can't be processed without this birth certificate. I don't mean to inconvenience anyone, but I have to ask on behalf of my son. Is there any way it could get reviewed while I am here? It would only take a minute, and would make all the difference in the world."

Tipping her head to one side, the clerk gives my plea some thought. She digs through the pile, and retrieves the application.

"My boss, Mrs. Ntembe, has an office on the second floor," she says, holding out the form. "I can't say for sure, but maybe she will be able to help you get it authorized by the registrar general today, if she's not too busy."

When Sharon and I arrive on the second floor we ask for directions to Mrs. Ntembe's office. We are informed that her office is down the hall, but that she has gone on a coffee break. After an hour she has still not returned. I trudge back down to the clerk's booth on the main floor.

"Is there anyone else that can help me? I can't find her."

"I've done what I can do," replies the clerk. "Just leave the form here and we will mail it to you when it is finished," she tells me, trying to maintain a patient tone.

"Tandela, if you wait for it to be mailed you could be waiting months," Sharon says quietly so the clerk doesn't hear. Again, I nervously tread upon the benevolence of the clerk.

"Is there another name of someone that I could talk to?" I ask. "I just need to know I've done all that I can to try to get it authorized today."

The clerk runs her hand through her meticulously groomed bob. Her eyes are not unfeeling and I hold my breath. She shrugs her shoulders. "The only other person I can think of is Barnabas Tororo. His office is on the third floor. I can't guarantee he will help you, but you can try."

Unfortunately, Mr. Tororo wants nothing to do with me or my problem.

"Who sent you?" he asks gruffly. His beady eyes glare at me under large eyebrows that have grown bushy with age. Close to retirement, he gives the impression that the last thing he wants to be bothered with is a task that is not on his list of official duties.

"The clerk at the front desk," I respond.

"She doesn't know what she is talking about. I don't handle these sorts of matters. Just leave it with the clerk and they will sort it out eventually, I'm sure." He waves us out.

"Eventually" is not good enough for me.

"Let's see if Mrs. Ntembe's back," Sharon suggests. We trudge down the stairs for what feels like the tenth time this morning. There is still no sign of the mysterious Mrs. Ntembe. The clock at the end of the hall shows that two hours have passed since we arrived. My eyes are drawn to the long thin hand that steadily ticks, a sharp reminder of how quickly the days are disappearing. Sharon is quiet, her eyes narrow with determination. I realize I have never seen her look so serious.

"Excuse me." She hurries up to a man that looks like he is part of the janitorial staff. The man leans toward her, resting his hands on his broom as she begins to speak to him in Luganda. He nods his head and gestures with one arm as he replies. After a short discussion, Sharon returns and leads me up to the third floor. From her beaming smile I can tell that she is pleased with the new information she has received.

"I told the man we had an appointment with the registrar general and were having difficulty finding her office." In response, the man gave her precise directions to the office of the registrar general, describing her as a "very powerful woman." I am more than a bit hesitant to go marching in unannounced to the office of one of the highest-ranking officials at the Ministry of Constitutional Affairs, but I am desperate. What else can I do? I stop outside her open office door, take a deep breath, and knock.

A heavyset African woman with impeccable hair, large gold earrings, and a bright pink blouse waves me in. She is seated behind a large pine desk cluttered with photo frames and stacks of paper. She extends a plump hand toward me, gesturing for the certificate. I hand it over and continue standing, anticipating that it will take no more than a few seconds for her to provide her signature.

"Have a seat."

Or maybe longer.

The registrar general squints at me through over-sized eyeglasses so intensely it is as though she is able to see my heart quicken with every beat inside my chest. I am beginning to suspect this may not be as straightforward as I anticipated. Not a word is spoken. The silence in the room grows more noticeable, and I become more and more uncomfortable.

When I first entered her office, I thought it would work in my favour that the registrar general was a woman. I figured that, likely a mother herself, she would be sympathetic to my plea for a birth certificate for a boy I hope will become my son.

She breaks the silence: "You people."

This does not sound promising.

"Always in a rush to get things done right away. You

think just because you are a foreigner, I will stamp this for you, here, this moment."

Perhaps she is not having a good start to her day.

"You think you are special? Well, you will not get special treatment here. No. Definitely not. I'll have to take my time and see if everything here is correct."

She slowly goes through the original form I had to fill out and cross-checks it with the certificate the clerk typed up. I feel like she is doing everything in her power to make me squirm, for she pauses painstakingly at every word. I bite my tongue. *Don't you dare say a word,* I tell myself. The last thing I need to do is further aggravate this woman.

"Okay, that will be one hundred dollars, please." She rests her chin in one hand while the other casually shuffles around some papers with feigned indifference.

"One hundred dollars American?" I repeat.

"Yes," she replies, her eyebrows raised over a challenging stare. American is always the currency quoted when dollars are mentioned. But there is not supposed to be any charge for her signature. And one hundred dollars is a significant sum. This has to be a bribe.

After I told her about the issue with the probation officer, Sharon warned me that I would encounter a lot of requests for bribes in the process of pursuing adoption. She said that paying bribes is a common way of getting things done, especially if you need something done quickly. And I do.

My mouth is dry. What am I supposed to say now? All that stands between me and the document I need to apply for Mark's passport is one hundred dollars. And I am thinking of refusing? Am I insane?

"I mean three hundred dollars. I misspoke," she says with a nonchalant wave of her hand.

Three hundred now? This is crazy! She can tell how badly I want this birth certificate. She knows what is at stake here. Perhaps she encounters people pursuing adoption all the time — couples who have already paid thousands of dollars and waited months, even years, to have their adoption finalized. A few hundred dollars would be considered nothing at the end of such an arduous journey.

We are interrupted by a phone call. While the registrar general is preoccupied with the call, I run through my options. I know this woman has the power to deny me the signature today and can also ensure I am refused at each future attempt. At the very least, her refusal to sign the birth certificate today will put a huge stall in the process. Even if everything goes as smoothly as possible from here on out, it is still going to be incredibly difficult to have a visa in place for Mark by the time I am supposed to leave the country.

On the other hand, while paying the bribe guarantees the birth certificate, it puts everything else in jeopardy. It is possible that down the road, if this interaction is exposed, it could be used by a judge to deny my adoption request on the basis that it reveals a compromise of integrity and ethics. It's horrible to think that after fostering Mark for the three-year trial period, someone will still have the power to yank him from my arms. That, as a three-year-old, even though he knows nothing other than life with Mommy Tandela, Mark could be forcibly separated from me and sent to an orphanage. This is a little boy we are talking about. He's worth all the money in the world to me. I'd give it all for this valuable documentation.

Corruption and adoption go hand in hand all over the world. This is part of the reason why, in many places, adoption is not only difficult for people overseas to navigate and afford, it is also increasingly inaccessible to local citizens. Many Ugandans dismiss the idea of legal adoption for the very reason that they cannot afford to jump through all the financial loopholes.

It would be so simple to give her the money. But how could indulging in corruption of any sort be consistent with God's will? If this adoption idea is really God's plan, I must believe he is big enough to bring it about without any illegal activity. *Lord, provide a way,* I silently pray. I want her signature more than anything. *Lord, bring this about in a way that honours you and Mark.* Mark is not property. He is a gift.

"Um, I don't believe there is a legitimate charge for this. I think this part is supposed to be free." The palms of my hands are damp with sweat, and a tingly sensation rushes over my arms as my heart rate rapidly increases again.

"Are you questioning me? Me? Well, maybe I won't stamp it after all."

Don't budge, Tandela, I tell myself. *Have faith. Hold your own. Have faith.*

"You think you can march in here and tell me how to do my job? You think you are better than me? You don't believe I work hard every day and think carefully about every document that passes my desk? I take this very seriously. I work very hard. And now I have to think over this for a moment. You need to really consider how much this means to you." She waves the certificate in the air in front of my face. *Oh, I know how much this means to me, lady.* And I have counted the cost of what I am about to say.

"I know you work very hard and you see a lot of people every day. I am just trying to make sure that everything I do is legal in the eyes of the law. Your approval of this certificate means the world to me, but I told myself from the beginning I was committed to making sure everything was done legally. I cannot risk doing anything under the table and—" I am interrupted by the ringing of her phone. Again.

My head feels strangely light and my stomach suddenly very queasy. Quick, shallow breaths provide insufficient oxygen to my fading body. The room seems to be closing in on me. My fingernails dig deep into my knee, resulting in a refreshing jolt of pain that brings everything into sharper focus. Fighting off a panic attack, I force myself to take ten deep breaths.

Sitting here alone, completely dependent on the mercy of this stranger, I yearn for the emotional support of a spouse. I long for a hand to hold and to be told that it is going to be okay. I wish there were someone to look out for me. Someone with whom I can suffer through the hurdles and also celebrate the victories. I'm too young to do this on my own. *I'm only twenty-two, remember, God?* All this would make more sense if I were married. The concrete floor meets my vacant stare, its surface hard and unfeeling.

A couple of minutes later, still engaged on the phone, the registrar general thrusts the birth certificate across her desk toward me. She has scribbled her name in blue ink at the bottom. It is official. I nod my head in appreciation and softly murmur "Thank you" before hurrying out of the office, fearful she may change her mind. I rush Sharon down the stairs and out of the building.

"We got it!" My cheeks are flushed with joy as I give her the good news.

"Oh, Tandela, that's wonderful!" Her arms reach out to hug me and I notice the corners of her eyes are wet with tears. "I'm so relieved. You were in her office for so long I was worried. What happened in there?"

I fill Sharon in on all that transpired with the registrar general once we are outside and beyond earshot of anyone in the building.

"I'm sorry it was so stressful, though I'm not entirely surprised with her demands," she admits with a grimace, shaking her head. "Anyway, what matters now is that you've got it. We need to get photocopies made right away."

Sharon leads me to a nearby store where we have copies made of the birth certificate and where I purchase a bright blue plastic folder for the documents' safekeeping. After a quick lunch we catch a bus back to Jinja. It is three o'clock in the afternoon when we arrive at the taxi park, and, eager to get started on Mark's passport application, I head to an internet café on my way to the orphanage to print out the application forms. Sharon has offered to travel with me back to Kampala this Sunday evening in order to hand in the application first thing Monday morning. Today is Thursday, which means there is only one business day for me to get everything organized.

Back at the orphanage, the children are outside finishing up their afternoon playtime. I duck under an assortment of cloth diapers hanging from the clothesline and hurry to Mark. He is sitting in the lap of one of the housemothers, clapping his hands with delight as a group of housemothers and older children sing and dance together. He slaps his knees with glee when he sees me approach. My sweaty, pale hands gently grasp his dark, dusty little fists, and I affectionately touch my nose to his, letting his eyelashes brush my cheeks. In this tender moment, as our faces meet, the stress and anxiety of the last two days fade into a distant memory. *It was all so worth it.*

Later that evening, once Mark falls asleep, I spread the passport forms out on our kitchen counter. I am pleased to discover that the forms are straightforward, and I am able to fill them out quickly. All I need to complete the application are passport photos for Mark and two signatures from guarantors. I will ask the probation officer and Margaret to be my guarantors.

It is nine o'clock in the evening when my cell phone rings.

"Tandela, it's Peter. How did things go in Kampala?" he asks.

"We managed to get Mark's birth certificate," I exclaim ecstatically, trying to keep my voice low so as not to wake Mark. "It was a lot more difficult than I thought. There's no way I would have been able to do it without Sharon's help." I fill him in on the challenges we faced at the police station and then at the Ministry of Constitutional Affairs.

"It's incredible you were able to get a birth certificate in one day," Peter marvels. "You may have been the first person to walk unannounced into the Registrar General's office," he says chuckling.

"What else was I going to do? I'm functioning in a time crunch. I had no choice. I'm going to go back to the passport office on Monday," I inform him. "I guess the next step after that is to apply for his visa at the Canadian Consulate in Kampala?"

"Yes, but I think you'll have a better chance of getting the visa completed in time if you go to the Canadian High Commission in Nairobi. The consulate in Kampala sends all the visa requests to Nairobi for authorization, and you have to eventually go to Nairobi in person for an interview. So you may as well just hand it in there and try to get the interview done at the same time."

Peter goes on to explain that he and Mary-Anne took this route with their second adoption, but learned the hard way that it only works if you have documentation from the Ugandan authorities that prove they are aware and supportive of your visa request.

"Otherwise the Kenyan government will suspect that you are trying to evade the Ugandan government and will refuse to process your request. That's what happened to us." I hear him sigh, remembering that disheartening verdict. "But I still recommend you go directly to Nairobi, because if you don't, it will never get done before you are set to leave for Canada in March. But it will only work this way if you have legitimate documentation that shows they can trust you. A lot of it is because of their concern with child trafficking," he adds.

I ask him how long Mark will be allowed to stay in Canada. He tells me that there is a space on the form for me to write how many months I would like the visa for, and advises that I only ask for a one-month visa.

"This is the safest thing to do, since it is much more likely that the High Commission will grant you a one-month visa over a six-month visa." He explains that once I am in Canada, I can apply to have the visa extended to six months.

Peter ends our conversation on a thoughtful note. "You know, I always wondered why both adoptions were so difficult for us, why we faced so many hurdles. I hope that the mistakes we made will turn out for your good, Tandela," he confides before hanging up the phone. "It will help me believe that there was a greater purpose behind the struggles."

After my phone call with Peter, I'm unable to sleep. I lie in bed, wondering what I can possibly give the Kenyan government to prove to them I am trustworthy and my request for a visa is legitimate. And not only legitimate, but supported by Ugandan authorities. I have so little time left, I can't afford to go all the way to Nairobi and be sent away, like Peter was.

Swinging my legs over the side of my bed, I gather the blue folder in my arms and head into the kitchen where I can turn on a light without disturbing Mark. I proceed to make a list of all the major grounds on which the authorities could refuse my request for a Canadian visa for Mark:

1. Child trafficking. They could argue that the reason I am taking the request to Kenya is to evade the Ugandan authorities because I am illegally abducting Mark.

2. How will they know I will return once Mark's visa expires? Peter told me the longest Mark will be allowed to stay in Canada is six months, so I'll need to provide proof that I am committed to returning to Uganda once Mark's visa is up.

3. Finances. Since I have no job at the present, they could argue I am financially unfit to provide for Mark in a country with a substantially higher cost of living.

The evening air is cool, and yet I am uncomfortably warm as I stare uneasily at the paper. Without the support of someone with a great deal of authority, my chances of getting a visa processed in Kenya do not look good. But who will vouch for me? Who of influence can attest to my plea for a visa for Mark? The probation officer is the only authority figure that I know personally, and not in a million years would he travel all the way to Kenya for this.

I quietly climb back into bed. My thin foam pillow provides little support for my head, which feels unusually heavy tonight. I shove my hands underneath for added cushion when an idea comes to mind. I will get the probation officer's support in the form of a letter. I will share my plan with him tomorrow when I request his signature as a guarantor for Mark's passport application.

THE NEXT MORNING, once the children have all been fed their breakfast, I go straight to the Department of Probation and Social Welfare. I bring Mark with me because afterward I am going to get his passport photos taken. I pray Mr. Makiywe is in his office. Since today is Friday, and I am planning on traveling to the passport office on Monday, if I don't get his signature on the application today, I will have to postpone my trip until later next week.

There is only one person in line ahead of us, which is a good sign; this means Mr. Makiywe must be in today. What a relief. While we wait, I walk up and down the outside hallway, gently bouncing Mark up and down while he sits in the baby carrier on my back.

Eventually we are called in. As Mr. Makiywe adds his signature to the passport application, I inform him of my plan to go straight to Kenya to get the visa and my need for a letter of support.

"Yes, I can sign such a letter," Mr. Makiywe tells me. He rests his elbows on his desk, his large biceps pulling his shirtsleeves taut as he crosses his arms. "But it would be much better if you had it endorsed by a judge instead."

"A judge?"

"Yes, a judge from the High Court in Jinja. That will carry much more weight than a letter from me."

I never would have guessed that Mr. Makiywe, of all people, would be the one to provide me with such valuable advice. Though I may not agree with how he does business, I have complete confidence that he is more aware than anyone I know of what kinds of things carry weight among African bureaucrats.

From Mr. Makiywe's office, Mark and I walk to a small convenience store in downtown Jinja for his passport photos. It takes a few minutes to get one with Mark looking straight at the camera, but eventually they tell me they have one that works and I can come back in the afternoon to pick it up. Margaret suggests I use the computer in her office to type up the letter for the judge during the afternoon naptime. As usual, a few of the babies are fussy today. I write the letter in quick bouts, rushing in and out of the dorm as I try to soothe the babies to sleep. Thankfully, the courthouse is only a ten-minute walk from the orphanage, so I will have time to print out the letter at the convenience store when I pick up Mark's passport photos on the way.

The large sign outside the main gate reads, "Courts of Judicature High Court Eastern Circuit." The property comprises a half-dozen or so single-storey white buildings topped with sloping red roofs. The area itself appears so informal that if not for the sign out front, I would doubt I was in the right place.

"I have a letter I need a judge to sign," I explain to the clerk at the front desk.

"You have a letter? What kind of letter?" she inquires.

"A letter regarding a visa application to the embassy in Kenya," I explain, handing her the letter.

"Mmm-hmm." She scans the letter. "Do you have an appointment?"

"No. But it will only take a minute," I add hurriedly.

"Unfortunately this is a very busy time for us. You can't just walk in and expect to see a judge," she informs me patiently. "I'm happy to make an appointment for you though." According to the clerk, the earliest I can get in is the following Wednesday at two o'clock. "Can you leave the letter here? It will allow the judge to review it prior to your appointment."

"Yes, of course. Thank you very much."

I would have preferred to see a judge today but am grateful the clerk was obliging, for I know my request is an unusual one. Besides, I do not need this letter immediately as I need to have Mark's passport before I can apply for his visa in Nairobi. In addition to the letter, I leave photocopies of my foster parent papers and Mark's birth certificate with the clerk.

Margaret writes me a letter stating that I am welcomed back at the orphanage whenever Mark's visa expires. I have no idea how long Mark will be allowed to stay in Canada if granted a temporary visa. This means I need to be prepared that our visit home may be a short one. We may end up living in Uganda for the rest of the three-year foster care period. My hope is that Margaret's letter will demonstrate to the visa office in Nairobi that, upon our return, I have a plan for our life in Jinja.

I now have to address the issue of my financial status. The authorities can legitimately use the fact that I have little money to my name as a reason to withhold a Canadian visa for Mark. To overcome this barrier, Mom and Dad offer to mail me statements proving their financial stability along with individual letters of support attesting to their desire to financially support Mark and me.

TODAY IS MONDAY, January 12th. It was difficult to say goodbye to Mark yesterday afternoon. Thankfully he didn't make a fuss when I left, probably because he is used to me having to juggle my time at the orphanage between him and the other children in my care. I've been told by the other housemothers that he's gone to bed quite easily at the orphanage on the nights I've been out of town, perhaps because he spent so many months at the orphanage prior to moving home with me.

He loves breakfast at the orphanage because he gets to drink porridge from a sippy cup, and this makes him feel independent. At ten months, he is crawling well, though he isn't what I would call a busy baby. He is content to sit for a long time if something interesting has caught his attention. Lately, his favourite activity is to pull himself up on things—usually my legs. With wobbling knees, he gazes up at me with his toothy grin, very satisfied with this newfound skill. After this trip, if all goes well, I will only have to leave him one more time when I travel to the visa office in Nairobi.

In Kampala, Sharon and I check out of our hostel,

the same Red Chilli Hideaway Hostel as last time, and take a taxi to the Department of Immigration, where we will hand in Mark's passport application. In the taxi I pull out the two passport photos we had taken in Jinja. Mark is wearing a white shirt that buttons just below his chin and is looking slightly to the left, where I was standing the moment the shot was taken. His mouth is gaping a little and I can catch a glimpse of his four bottom teeth. The camera leaves two light reflections on his cheeks and one on his forehead. His eyes are big and dark and perfect.

Dirt mixed with gravel crunches under the wheels of the taxi as it pulls over to the side of the road. The distinct scent of hay is a welcome contrast to the gritty car exhaust that fills the air. Towering above my head is an impenetrable stone wall that encircles the entire compound. A young parking attendant in a bright orange vest patrols the area, intent on ensuring that no one parks here for free. Outside the compound, street vendors sell passport holders as well as a variety of random trinkets.

"Where are you going?" the guard stationed at the main gate politely inquires. He is dressed head to toe in khaki military garb, and a large rifle casually hangs from his shoulder.

"To process a passport." I try to keep the anxiety I feel from creeping into my voice. He directs us to take our first left. We pass through another gate and find ourselves in a courtyard. A large canopy occupies the centre of the courtyard, providing shade to the rows and rows of chairs beneath, all of which are occupied. A number of people stand off to the side, seeking refuge wherever possible from the bright rays of the rising sun. The courtyard is enclosed by a perimeter of offices, each one consisting of a wooden door and barred windows. Rust on the tin roofs imitates the red dirt underfoot. Above one office a sign reads "Passport Control Officer." I have no idea where I am supposed to drop off the application, but this sounds like it might be a good place to start. I knock on the door. Nothing.

"Knock louder," suggests Sharon, motioning to the door. I knock again.

"Yes, come in," booms a deep voice. I turn the handle and peek inside. A man around my father's age stands up from behind his desk, one arm pushing his chair back while the other waves us in.

"I'm here to hand in a passport application," I begin.

"I have been expecting you," he says with a kind nod. He is dressed in the same uniform as the guard out front but thankfully no rifle hangs from his shoulder. Through the corner of my eye, I can tell that Sharon is just as surprised as I am by his reply.

"He must think I am someone else," I murmur under my breath, unsure of how to proceed.

"The passport is for your foster child, correct? I think his name is Mark?"

I stand there speechless, my mouth gaping open in astonishment, as the gentleman informs me that Peter, whom he knows well, called him this past Friday after speaking with me on Thursday evening. Peter explained my situation and mentioned that it would be helpful if, when I arrived here on Monday, I could have the passport processed as soon as possible.

"May I see the forms, please?"

I pull out my blue folder and hand him the application and the photos. He carefully examines each page.

"Everything looks good," he says. "Come back this afternoon and it will be ready. You can pay when you pick it up."

I cannot believe what I just heard.

"Today? This afternoon? Are you serious?"

"Peter is a good man. I'm happy I can do this for him." His fingers tap the file with certainty.

This is a miracle. It usually takes three weeks to have a passport made, and instead I am getting Mark's processed in one day.

In the late afternoon, with the passport tucked securely in my folder, Sharon and I head back to Jinja, filled with joy at what transpired at the passport office. The road leading out of Kampala is noisy and traffic-jammed, and our matatu driver is heavy on his brakes, but everything seems peaceful to me. In fact, the chaos outside seems a distant world away as my mind dwells on the beautiful truth that I now have a passport for Mark.

My fingers skim over the smooth, dark blue fabric. On the front cover is the Ugandan coat of arms — a shield, a crane, and an antelope. Under the figures is a banner with the words "For God And My Country." These words are a humble reminder of God's providence and how he has answered my prayers for this situation. Many times I've doubted he would produce the required paperwork on such a tight timeline. Yet, despite my doubts, God has continued to bestow unmerited grace and mercy on me.

Two days later it is Wednesday, the day of my appointment with the judge in Jinja. After a nerve-racking hour in the waiting room, I am led into the judge's chambers. Laid out on her desk is the letter I wrote with the photocopied documents that support my case. Taking care to avoid eye contact so as not to appear rude, I comply with her request that I take a seat. The scolding I received at the Ministry of Constitutional Affairs is at the forefront of my mind. Is this woman going to be equally hard on me? The judge holds up a picture frame containing a photo of a group of children, enough to make up a soccer team.

"You want to adopt a child?" Though she is smiling, her eyes are cold. "I have children, too. I have eleven children," she says, pointing to the photo. I begin to feel nauseated. Experience tells me why this woman is bringing up her large family, and it is not to boast of her fertility. It is about money.

The judge continues on. "You know, I have so many kids I can't afford all their school fees. Children are expensive, as you will see. Yes, we mothers must help one another." She pauses, waiting to hear how I am going to respond. I do my best to maintain a clueless expression, pretending I have no idea of what she is insinuating, though I know without a doubt she is implying a bribe be paid.

A long silence ensues, making me incredibly uncomfortable. Eventually the judge looks up from her desk. With disbelieving eyes, she gives me a look that says, "You'll not get far, but who am I to stop you now?" Begrudgingly she picks up her pen, enjoys a long, dramatic pause with her hand in the air, and brings it down on the paper, giving the document her much-needed flowery signature.

Once out of the judge's chambers, I stop, noticing she has replaced my letter with her own. It reads:

To Whom It May Concern:
Re: Permission To Travel Outside Uganda With a Foster Child

This is to certify that TANDELA LYNNE SWANN has been granted permission to travel outside of Uganda with Mark Kirab Swann, her foster child, as per care application No. 0231/2003.

Tandela was granted legal foster care of the abandoned baby boy Mark. It is therefore the decision of this court that she be permitted to take Mark with her on her travels to Canada as she was already granted an order to foster on the 16th day of December, 2003.

Janet Bakulima
Family and Children's Court/Jinja

I am elated, for I believe I now have everything I need to make a strong case for Mark's visa application in Kenya. But I have little time to celebrate. When Mark woke up this morning it was evident that he was suffering from another serious eye infection. He is at the orphanage now, but he needs medical attention. I know from past experience with him that this infection is not going to go away on its own. I phone my mom, needing her advice as a physician. I describe Mark's eye condition to her. She listens carefully, then tells me the type of antibiotics she thinks he needs and advises that they be given through an IV.

The hospital, as usual, is inundated with children. Since it is severely understaffed, it takes hours for us to finally see a nurse. I explain that the cream they prescribed in the past has proved ineffective and ask the nurse to consider IV antibiotics. She leaves to consult with a doctor and returns one hour later, needle in hand. I lay Mark down on the bed. The nurse prods his tiny arm for a vein. In addition to Mark being so small and weak, his dark skin makes it very difficult to find a suitable vein into which she can insert the needle. First poke. Mark screams. He writhes on the bed, trying to get away. Second poke. He flares his body around and kicks the nurse in the groin.

"Mark, sweetie, it's okay," I say. But nothing I do reassures him.

"I can't do this," the nurse says, defeated. "Now he is too frightened of me." She hands me the needle. "You do it."

"Excuse me?" My eyes widen in astonishment.

"I will hold him. He is less afraid of you than me." I have never inserted an IV into anyone in my life, nor do I ever want to, especially into someone I love, like Mark.

"I can't. I have no idea how to do it." I can hear the panic in my voice, my heartbeat suddenly in my ears.

"You just have to find a vein. Just find a vein and push it in." The nurse holds out the needle. Her eyes are stern. I can tell from her no-nonsense expression that she's not going to have another go. Mark's wrist is beginning to show bruising from her previous attempts.

"Mark, this is going to be quick, okay?" I look into his eyes. They are full of fear. I have very little time before Mark realizes what I am about to do. I must do this quickly.

"It's going to help you feel all better, and then your eye won't hurt anymore." I continue talking while I sleuth for a vein. I think I see one.

Deep breath.

Poke.

Scream.

It's in.

The nurse quickly secures it to his arm with tape, hooks it up to the drip, and covers it with a tensor bandage. Together we sit until the full first round of antibiotics has gone into his system.

"Bring him back in three days for a second dose," the nurse advises. "The full treatment will take about two weeks. And don't let him take that IV needle out."

At Mom's suggestion, for the duration of the treatment, I fashion a sock to Mark's good hand to prevent him from scratching at the needle. Thankfully, the antibiotics take effect and Mark recovers, growing stronger with each passing day.

CHAPTER EIGHT

February 2004, Uganda & Kenya

TODAY IS February 15th, and I leave this afternoon on an overnight bus for Nairobi, Kenya, where I hope to receive a Canadian visa for Mark. The trip will take about fifteen hours, and, since the bus leaves at four thirty in the afternoon, this will put me in Nairobi by early morning.

I lay Mark down on his back, a cloth diaper in my hand. He will go down for a nap now and will hopefully be asleep when I leave the orphanage in an hour for the Jinja bus depot. After I change him, I run my hand up and down his tummy, his dark skin shining ever so slightly from the Vaseline I rubbed all over his body after his bath this morning. Nothing makes Mark laugh like being tickled. His giggles rise and fall as he squirms with delight under my dancing fingers. I carry him across the room and quietly lay him down in the crib he uses for his daytime naps at the orphanage, one that he shares with another baby who is already fast asleep.

I continue our usual pre-nap routine, gently running my hand up and down his cheeks, a habit that helps his body relax. Within minutes his eyes close and his lower jaw slackens. It pains me to leave him, but I have no choice. Since it is already mid-February, going to Nairobi is the only chance I have to get a Canadian visa for him before my flight on March 8th. I would have preferred to travel by plane to Nairobi from Kampala, as this would make for a shorter trip, but the flights are expensive.

As I wander around the rustic bus depot, my heart starts to quicken. I know I must board soon, yet my nerves are getting the best of me thinking about the terrible automobile accident that Solomon, the orphanage's guard, was in this past week. He was traveling with a group of friends to Kampala in a matatu when their vehicle was sideswiped by a semi-truck. Everyone in the matatu was killed except for Solomon, who suffered two fractured ribs and a dislocated shoulder. I can't help but be reminded of my brother Nathan, and how in the accident involving his friends, there was only one survivor out of seven. I hope that Solomon will be able to come back to work soon, if only to give him a purpose for getting out of bed each morning.

Even before Solomon's accident, I was filled with anxiety about traveling by bus, what with the deteriorating quality of Kenya's roads, the unpredictability of the drivers of the various matatus, motorcycles and automobiles, and the declining condition of the buses built years and years ago, without seat belts — not to mention the frequent highway robberies.

The Akamba bus line, the one I will be taking, offers two different routes into Kenya. The two parallel bus routes take approximately the same time and each offer a number of stops along the way, allowing passengers to choose their bus based on whichever puts them closest to their destination. Since both terminate in Nairobi, it doesn't matter to me which one I choose. Either one promises a long, boring, and lonely trip.

"Mama Tandela!" a voice calls out amid the commotion in the overcrowded station. I can hardly believe there is another woman also named Tandela boarding a bus nearby.

"Mama Tandela!" I can't help but smile to myself as I make my way onto the bus. I've never met anyone who shares my name. The person yells again, louder this time. I turn as I hand my ticket to the driver. Who is this other Tandela? And then I see Rose, a housemother from the orphanage, furiously waving her hands in the air trying to get my attention. She beckons for me to join her in line for the other bus traveling to Nairobi via Busia.

"Excuse me, I am going to go on the other bus," I hastily apologize to the driver, hurrying out the front doors with my grey and red backpack slung over my shoulder. Made for camping or trekking, my pack can hold up to forty-five litres, but at the moment it is practically empty since I'm planning on being in Nairobi for only three or four days. As if I do not stand out enough already, my bag screams "tourist."

"What a surprise!" I cry breathlessly, as I sling my arm around her and squeeze her shoulders. "I didn't know you were going to Kenya today."

Here I am, at a bus station thirteen thousand kilometres from home, and I just happen to be traveling to Kenya at the same time as one of the few people

I know in Jinja. What a joy! I'm so happy to have a traveling companion.

"I have family near Nairobi that I am visiting for one week," she explains, leading me onto the bus. "It is safer toward the back," Rose continues as I follow her down the aisle. "But if you sit in the very back the ride is very uncomfortable. It's like being on the end of a whip, you get tossed around so much. How about you, what are you doing in Nairobi?" she asks, settling into her seat.

"It's for Mark. I'm going to the Canadian Embassy there because I'm trying to get a visa for him so that he can come home with me in March and meet my family." Rose, like everyone at the orphanage, knows of my hope to adopt Mark. Yet other than Sharon and Margaret, I haven't shared many of the details with anyone else.

"I see how Mark is with you," Rose says, smiling broadly. "He clings to you like a son to his mother. That's how he thinks of you, as his mother. I remember when he first came to us, he was so little and so sick," she says, shaking her head solemnly at the memory.

As we pull out of the bus depot, Rose tells me that there are not enough children's homes to care for all the Ugandan orphans. She admits that it is far better for a child to have a home and a family than to live in an orphanage. However, she adds that it's the children who have no one to care for them, those who aren't in an orphanage, who are the worst off.

"When I see little children living in the village dumps or on the streets, it makes me so sad," she elaborates. "They have no one to look after them. That's why they run around in little packs like dogs."

The bus continues to fill up as we make routine stops outside of Kampala. January and February, the two hottest months of the year, are popular months to travel because of the favourable weather. On this night bus, however, there will not be much for us to see other than the headlights of oncoming traffic.

"You must be careful in Nairobi," Rose holds up her index finger for emphasis. "It is much more dangerous than Kampala. My cousin, the last time he traveled on a bus from Nairobi to Kampala, was robbed by a group of bandits posing as passengers. No one was hurt, they just wanted money," she taps my knee reassuringly. "And make sure not to go north of River Road; that's not a safe area."

"North of River Road," I repeat, committing it to memory. I cringe slightly at the realization I forgot to pack a map.

"You go there as a tourist and you are fair game, they say," Rose continues. "But Nairobi is much better than it used to be. You used to hear many stories about people whose hands were cut off with one clean swipe of a machete, just for the sake of a watch." With wide eyes she shakes her head in disbelief, her black braids swinging side to side.

She changes topics abruptly, as though trying to distract me from her previous statement. "Do you know where you are staying?"

When she learns that I haven't made reservations anywhere, she offers to help me find a hostel near the visa office. I'm immensely grateful to her for this and for how our conversation has momentarily taken my mind off my worries. I'm not only anxious about getting to Nairobi accident-free, I also have concerns about getting across the border because I don't have a travel visa for Kenya.

Back when I was in Canada applying for my Ugandan visa, I obviously had no clue that God was going to have me travel to Kenya, and definitely not for the purpose of securing a visa to bring a baby home with me. If I had applied for one from Uganda, there is little likelihood I would have received it in time anyway. I'd been reassured by a couple of people that it shouldn't be a big deal, but now I'm regretting not looking into it a bit more thoroughly. The prospect of being refused entry to Kenya and getting kicked off the bus in the middle of nowhere is frightening. And then, if I am let in, there is the issue of being allowed back into Uganda. My visa for Uganda is a single entrance visa, which means I am supposed to enter Uganda only via the Entebbe Airport. There is no guarantee that I will be allowed back in via the Busia border crossing. I clench my hands together in my lap and silently pray that God will protect our bus from harm and for the Kenyan authorities to have mercy on me.

At six o'clock we pull up to the Uganda–Kenya border. We file out of the bus and line up outside to face the customs officers. What if they deny me entry? Nobody else appears to have a reason to be concerned, for everyone but me looks like they were born in Uganda or Kenya.

"Where do you live?" The officer barely glances at Rose as she hands him her identification.

"Jinja," she replies.

"And what do you do in Jinja?"

"I work at a children's home."

"And where are you traveling to in Kenya?" He studies her face, taking care to note whether or not it matches the photo on her identification card.

"Nairobi. That's where my family lives. I'm going for a visit."

"Very well, have a good trip." The officer waves her along. "Next." I approach the booth and hand over my Canadian passport.

"You are from Canada?" the officer inquires.

"Yes," I confirm.

"What are you doing in Uganda?"

"I am volunteering at the same children's home as Rose," I reply, pointing ahead to where Rose is waiting for me.

When border officials question a white person, they generally receive one of two responses as to why the person has traveled here: either for aid work or for tourism. I hope this response will satisfy the officer so I don't have to go into further detail of why I am really going to Kenya. I'm not sure it will help my case for him to know that I am seeking a visa to bring a Ugandan baby back home to Canada with me.

"And where are you traveling to?"

"Nairobi."

"And what business do you have in Nairobi?" How I wish I could say I am visiting friends, or doing a volunteer stint with the Red Cross, or perhaps interning with the United Nations. These are all very respectable and straightforward answers, whereas the truth is so much more complicated and may very well cast a wave of suspicion over me.

"I'm going to the Canadian Embassy to get a traveler's visa for my son," I quickly reply. The officer studies me, trying to decide if I am serious. Desperate to add legitimacy to my case, I hand him Mark's passport. I am comforted by the fact that I also have the letter from the High Court judge that, if needed, will add to my story's credibility.

He flips it open and reads aloud, "Mark Kirab Swann. Born March 11th, 2003. Country of birth: Uganda."

"This is your son?" he asks, his mouth downturned in confusion. The date of Mark's birth as indicated in his Ugandan passport is seven months earlier than my entrance into Uganda.

"He is my foster son," I elaborate. "I want to adopt him but I have to foster him for three years first. I'm trying to get a visa so we can go back to Canada together to visit my family and begin the adoption paperwork."

The officer stares at me, taking in my appearance. I can only guess what he sees as I haven't looked in a mirror for a while. My mascara is probably smudged from falling asleep on the way here. I must have noticeable bags under my eyes, from long days at the orphanage and tending to Mark at night. And I'm probably not doing a very good job at hiding my nerves. At least my hair, braided in cornrows, stays in place.

"Good luck," he says with a nod, and waves me on. Elated, I join Rose in the lineup to reboard the bus, which is now on the Kenyan side of the border. My steps feel light and effortless.

I am one step closer to bringing Mark home.

After a quick stop for some food, I refasten my seat belt, the presence of which brings me great comfort, allowing me to sleep more soundly. The seat belts look very new and must have been installed recently in anticipation of Kenya's plan to initiate a national policy of seat belts in all buses and matatus. I lean back in my seat and close my eyes, now free from any apprehensions about the border crossing. The rest of the trip should be uneventful. I drift off to sleep, expecting that I won't be roused for hours until we enter the hustle and bustle of Nairobi.

I AM JOLTED awake by terrified screams. My eyes open to blackness.

"Get off the bus! Get off!" a voice hollers frantically. I can't see who is yelling, but the sound is emanating from the front of the bus. *Our driver?* I try to focus. "There has been an accident! Leave all your belongings and exit now!" he yells with great urgency.

The overhead lights click on, and my adjusting night vision is instantly lost. Rose rubs her frightened eyes, as unaware as I of what exactly is going on. Adrenaline shoots through me and I am suddenly wide awake, panic setting in as I hear hysterical screams and intense shouts from every direction. Mayhem erupts in the aisle as a crowd of confused and agitated travelers compete with each other to set foot on solid ground. In all the uproar, I get separated from Rose.

Outside, the noise is amplified. *What is going on?* A number of people are running away from the bus down the road, and I crane my neck in their direction. In the darkness of the night, the light from a nearby flashlight offers a sudden glimpse of the devastating wreckage. A bus is lodged upside down in a ditch on the left-hand side of the road. Threatening billows of grey smoke surge from under the front hood. One after another, people are thrust outside the bus through windows. And judging by a few piles of bodies, some are already dead. I turn my cell phone on and use the little light it offers to guide me as I approach.

"We must get the survivors out immediately," a loud voice bellows above a sea of wailing. Near the front of the overturned bus, an elderly lady is trapped upside-down by her seat belt. I reach through the window, grasping with one hand to try to find the buckle. The woman does not speak. I touch her hand and it is cold. She is unconscious, if she is even still alive.

"Help!" My voice cracks with panic as my fingers frantically grope for the release button.

Two men are immediately at my side, and together we try to dislodge the woman from the bus. Because the front of the bus is so badly damaged, there is no way in or out except through the windows. Another man joins the rescue effort, and I move out of the way. One man climbs on the shoulders of another so that he can reach farther inside the bus. I walk away slowly. The glow from my phone illuminates ground darkened by blood and strewn with bodies. By now a chain of people are assembled between the two buses, and all of the surviving passengers are being loaded on to our bus.

I start to experience chills. Am I going into shock or just sweating from exertion? I look down at my hands. They are shaking. And blurry. I glance up to watch the chaos fade in and out of focus. A woman, one of the survivors, is being carried toward my bus. She has a deep gash on her forehead. I must be losing my mind because this woman looks familiar to me. But where could I have seen her?

And then it comes flooding back to me.

The turmoil surrounding me is forced into the background as the truth of what has happened imposes itself on me. Sounds that previously assaulted my ears are replaced with a ringing silence. I am vaguely aware that everything continues to advance violently forward, and yet I cannot move. I squeeze my eyes shut, hoping to regain my focus, and when I open them I see the woman disappear as she is lifted into the bus.

She was on the first bus I had almost boarded.

That wrecked bus was the bus I had originally chosen to take me to Nairobi. And yet, against all odds, Rose spotted me among all the other people at the bus station and called me off that bus to join her. Rose was an intervention by God, a miracle that may very well have saved my life.

IT IS NOW half past ten in the morning, three hours later than the bus was scheduled to arrive in Nairobi. It took over two hours to load the surviving passengers onto our bus before dropping them off at the Kenyatta

National Hospital. Rose has walked me to a hostel, and after ensuring I am settled, gives me a long hug goodbye.

"It is going to be okay," she says. "I trust you are going to get what you came here for. God has brought you here safely, and he will continue to protect you and provide for you." Behind her weary eyes I see a trace of the resilience that I have always admired in Sharon. Promising to see me in a week back at the orphanage, she waves and departs.

Conveniently located in downtown Nairobi on the second storey of a strip mall, the hostel is long and skinny with rooms off the main hallway. I change into the only other outfit I have, a pair of white capris and a black sleeveless shirt, and I touch up my makeup to look as respectable as possible. I stare back at myself in the mirror. It feels strange to just change clothes and keep going after such a traumatic experience, as though nothing has happened. And yet I must. I only have four days here in Nairobi. After double-checking that the plastic folder with all my precious documents is in my purse, I head downstairs.

"Can I help you find anything in Nairobi?" asks the gentleman in the check-in area. He is tidying up a stack of magazines.

"Yes, if you wouldn't mind. I need directions to the High Commission of Canada office."

"I see. You have a problem they need to help you with?" His tone is casual, and yet his inquiring eyes and raised eyebrows betray his curiosity.

"Well, kind of." I can tell his interest is growing. "I need to get a visa from them," I elaborate, "and have to go for an in-person interview."

"I see, okay." He pulls out a flimsy map from behind his desk. "This is where we are, see?" He draws a circle around an intersection. "And this is where the Canadian High Commission is." His finger rests in between two streets. "This is where you want to go. It will take maybe thirty minutes to walk." He hands the map to me. "You are going tomorrow?"

"No, I am going there right now," I respond, trying to sound confident for my own sake.

"Do you have an appointment?"

"No, but I'm hoping they'll see me anyway, or if not I'll at least make an appointment for tomorrow."

He shakes his head. "You won't get in today. You have to be there very early in the morning if you want anyone to see you. They'll be full now."

"But it's only ten thirty in the morning," I incredulously respond.

"Yes. But I have worked here for seven years, and do you know how many people have come in and out of these doors needing something from the High Commission? And unless they are waiting for the doors to open first thing in the morning, they come back empty-handed and very sad. So, I say to you"—here he emphatically taps his desk with the palms of his hands—"go early tomorrow, wait at the doors, and you will not come back empty-handed." Aware of my disappointment, he quickly adds, "But there is much to do in Nairobi."

He swiftly moves his fingers around the map, showing me all the things I can see and do in Nairobi to pass the time. But his suggestions fall on deaf ears. I have no interest in exploring Nairobi. I have nothing against the city, but I can concentrate on nothing other than my purpose in coming here. I'm in business mode, and there's no way I can just switch into tourist mode for the rest of the day.

I end up spending a large portion of the day at a restaurant that specializes in fried chicken. I sit there for hours, rehearsing answers to possible questions I may be asked during the visa interview and going over every document in the application until I know them all by heart. My application is many pages long, mainly because I have included a number of supporting documents. I have the letter from Margaret that guarantees I'll have a position back at the orphanage when Mark's Canadian visa expires, the letter of support from the judge, extensive financial statements that prove Mom and Dad have more than enough money to provide for us until I became financially independent, and a letter of support from Mom and Dad. I stare at their signatures. The sight of their handwriting makes me homesick. Their unwavering support at every step is an incredible blessing. I'm sure they have had many conversations behind closed doors about the situation, but when speaking to me they have been nothing but encouraging.

I read over their letter:

This letter is in regards to Mark Kirab Swann and his foster-parent Tandela Lynne Swann. I, Dr. David Swann and I, Dr. Laureen Swann commit to financially supporting Tandela Swann and Mark Swann for their six month stay in Canada should Mark's visa request be accepted. We willfully commit to covering any costs that extend Tandela's means, should this be necessary. We are in full understanding that the granting of a visitor visa for Mark to Canada allows him to visit Canada temporarily. We understand that when this visa expires Mark and Tandela will return to Uganda.

"Tandy," my mom's voice echoes in my ears. "If you get denied a visa for Mark, we will fight it. I will fight it from here, and you will fight it there. We will make it work." My mom has always been determined, and right now I am so thankful that God made her no other way.

A TAXI DROPS me off at the High Commission at seven o'clock the following morning. The office is located in a wealthy residential area of Nairobi. I stand on my tiptoes, but the cement wall lining the property towers above, preventing a glimpse of what lies within. I am alone except for a pigeon, which enjoys an exclusive view from a string of barbed wire atop the wall. Others join me over the course of the next thirty minutes, until a security guard approaches the gate. He unlocks it and ushers us through.

I walk down a long concrete driveway. Shafts of light from the morning sun, its yellow rays bright but not yet too hot, beam down on the lofty palm trees that border the road. Because the office is located in a neighbourhood rather than the central business district, the compound is devoid of the constant echo of car horns, making it strangely quiet. The driveway ends in a roundabout at the entrance to the building. We file up to a guard who sits in a black booth in front of the main doors.

"What are you here for?" His tone, though not impolite, suggests he takes his role of overseeing all who enter and exit the building seriously.

"I am here regarding a visa application I need processed." He presses down on a buzzer that unlocks the front door and waves me through. A large flight of stairs leads up from the entrance to a security station where a guard scans me with a metal detector and goes through all the contents in my bag. Next, I'm sent down a different set of stairs that leads to an outside courtyard. Open cubicles and interview rooms fill the courtyard and make up the ground level perimeter, while the second storey is composed of fully enclosed individual offices. There is a waiting area in the centre of the courtyard: a cluster of chairs shielded from the sun under a tent.

I walk up to the first employee I see and inquire about obtaining a visa. Since I am the first visitor, he shows me to one of the many nondescript cubicles himself.

"Hello, how can I help you?" The officer behind the desk is sharply dressed in a dark blue uniform of dress pants, collared shirt, and sports jacket.

"I have a visa application I need processed for my son." I try to exude confidence. "I mailed the application a few weeks ago, and I'm here for the interview portion."

"I see. And you have an appointment?"

"No, not yet." Hope is etched into the lines on my face as I force an optimistic smile.

"You must make an appointment for this sort of issue. You can hand in a copy of your application to me and when we get to it we will call you to set up an appointment," he informs me matter-of-factly.

When we get to it? They will never get to it before I am scheduled to fly home in two and a half weeks. What am I supposed to say in response to this? I don't think God spared me from the bus accident only to be told that I won't be able to get a visa in time. I wearily shift my weight from one foot to the other. I didn't sleep well last night, fighting off nightmares about the accident. I look up at the ceiling, tipping my head back to keep my tears at bay.

"Where are you traveling from, miss? Are you residing in Nairobi?" the officer asks, taking in my distress.

"I am living in Jinja. I took the bus here. I can only stay a couple of days," I add softly, my voice shaking with emotion.

"Hmm." He begins to flip through an appointment book on his desk. I watch his finger slide down the page, then stop. He looks up at me. "I think we can set one up for tomorrow." I take a deep breath. This is wonderful news. Nothing could be better except... getting an interview today.

"Is there any way that I can get one today?" I cringe as the words spill out of me before I have a chance to think them through.

"Miss, we need time to look over your application first. You can come back tomorrow at nine o'clock or you can come back in a month. Your choice."

I quickly hand over the application. "Tomorrow at nine will be fine. Thank you very much." The officer gives me a courteous nod, and I detect a glimmer of compassion in his eyes. I slowly turn away and retrace my steps toward the exit, hoping with all my heart that when I leave here tomorrow it will be with good news.

FOR THE SECOND night in a row, I sit alone on my bed at the hostel. I just finished leafing through a local newspaper and read that twelve people died in the bus accident two days ago. It was reported that the bus crashed because the driver was attempting to avoid a massive pothole. In the nightmare I had last night, I was back at the scene of the accident, surrounded by distressed passengers and wounded bodies.

Tonight all of the other guests are socializing in the common room. Most of the people are tourists stopping through on their way to a safari. Lonely as I am, I do not feel like being around strangers. I would rather be alone in my room than engage in an awkward conversation about why I happen to be in Nairobi.

I stretch out on my bed, my body unusually heavy, as though my anxiety is now manifesting itself in physical weight. The braids that fall halfway down my back are slightly bumpy under my head. As I rub my hand over them, I can feel that they are starting to get a bit fuzzy around my scalp. Getting my hair braided a month ago has meant I haven't had to think about styling my hair. I usually don't mind spending time on my hair and makeup, but for the past couple of months I have hardly had a minute to think of such things, or even look in the mirror.

The quiet and stillness of the room, with no crying babies to attend to and no Mark to look after, is unfamiliar to me. Having no immediate chores makes me feel almost lost; it has been so long since I have had an evening to myself. And yet I'm not sure if I welcome this quiet and stillness because it forces me to be completely alone with my thoughts — thoughts of the adoption and all the things I have no control over. Even if I am granted Mark's visa tomorrow, I am still just beginning the arduous task of convincing a number of authorities that I am fit to parent. And I am at the tip of the iceberg when it comes to the monstrosity of immigration paperwork that every prospective adoptive parent faces.

I know I should be thankful for securing an interview tomorrow. I should feel encouraged. But I don't. I long to escape to a place where my mind has no worries. It was less than a year ago that I graduated from university ready to take on the world, but I feel like a very different person now. Over the past four months I have been affected by a number of firsts. Not only have I become totally responsible for a child whom I cannot bear to live without, I have become friends with people who embody a strength and resilience I have not encountered before, met people whose lives have been devastated by war, and become accustomed to standing up to intimidating authority figures.

My faith has also changed with the tremendous

highs and lows of the past months. I arrived in Uganda confused about where to live, and then I found the perfect place in Jinja. My heart broke for an extremely sick little baby, and then my heart filled further still with love for him, more than I could ever imagine. I wrestled with the call to pursue adoption for him, but when I fully surrendered in obedience, I felt a tremendous peace.

I've faced situations where it seemed I was going to be denied the document I desperately needed, only to have it miraculously granted. Never in my life have I had to depend so deeply on the miraculous workings of God. I often think that my faith is stronger now than it has ever been before, but then I encounter moments of doubt that make me wonder if I have any faith at all. No matter how many miracles God performs, I still sometimes struggle to believe that God is always with me and is sovereign over all things. Tonight is one of those nights. Inside, where I want to have complete trust in God's goodness and power, I feel hollow.

Just as romantic feelings alone are unable to sustain a marriage though trying times, one's faith in God will crumble if it is based only on emotion. I know that God has revealed himself to me and has gifted me with faith in him, yet never have I found it so hard to believe. I tell myself to focus on the truth that God is good, he loves Mark, and he loves me.

But still I doubt.

My mind wanders to the possible scenarios that could take place at the end of the three-year foster period. What if, after everything, a judge denies me legal adoption rights? And Mark is taken away from me forever? From the one person in the world he trusts? It would be the ultimate act of betrayal. I wouldn't be able to convey, in a way that he would understand, that it's not my choice, that I am being forced to leave him.

Stop it! I tell myself. *Stop feeding yourself these ridiculous lies!*

But I can't. I begin to wonder if I have made all this up, the whole "I feel called to adopt Mark" thing. Did I really hear from God? Is he there at all? I draw my knees to my chest and, curled up on my bed in the fetal position, try to fend off the lies.

I try to cling to what I know to be true. Apart from God, there is no explanation for my attachment to Mark. Nothing other than a supernaturally derived love can account for the way my heart feels so full it could burst when Mark gazes into my eyes with a big grin, or the deep joy I experience when Mark stretches out his arms, wanting me to hold him. There is no rational explanation for the profound affection that drives a willingness to get up with him night after night, again and again, if that is what is required, and to care for him for years to come.

But if God is God, and God is good, why does he allow so much pain in the world? Why does he allow babies to be conceived and brought into the world in the darkest of circumstances? Why would he "knit Mark in his mother's womb" only to have him be discarded in the bottom of an outhouse? Is he good but lacking in power, too weak to carry out what he wants to do? If he were stronger, he could make things better. Surely he would redeem things.

I am kneeling on the bed in the midst of my thoughts, when from the depths of my memory specific conversations, sermons, and books are brought forth as though to confront these very doubts that threaten to overtake me. Rather than leaving me to fight alone, in this instance I sense God using seeds planted in my past to carry me through this crisis of faith. I remember the words that Moses said to Joshua before he died, words meant to encourage him and equip him, for God had chosen Joshua as the one who was to lead the Israelites into the Promised Land: "The LORD himself goes before you and will be with you; he will never leave you nor forsake you. Do not be afraid; do not be discouraged" (Deuteronomy 31:8).

God reminds me of his Word, the truth. He did redeem the world. And he looks at me, a child of God, in the same way that I look at Mark. *You are my daughter. I am fiercely protective of you. I love you unconditionally,* God tells me. *All of those maternal emotions you have for Mark are founded in me. This is what I meant when I said that I made man in my image.*

Tandela, all is not lost. I did send a Redeemer. I sent my Son, Jesus. It was the only way to bring reconciliation to a world that is fallen. Jesus picked up the pieces for you — for everyone — because you could never do it yourself. No matter how hard you tried, you could not put the world back together as it should be. Jesus took all that was sinful and destructive and bore it on his body when he was nailed to the cross. And through this excruciating suffering that Jesus willingly endured, grace was made victorious over sin. Yes, my daughter, suffering without a purpose is disheartening. But take heart. Though you may not understand the mystery of these words during your time on earth, I need you to believe that I have allowed suffering to exist for a purpose. And my purpose is always good.

THE NEXT MORNING I report for my interview at the High Commission at eight thirty. At nine twenty-five my name is called over the loudspeaker and I am escorted into a vacant room. It is approximately eight feet wide by ten feet long. The surrounding beige walls are bare but for an old grey surveillance camera bolted to the ceiling in one corner, recording my every move. The room, cold and without windows, is unnervingly similar to a police interrogation room.

"Have a seat here, Miss Swann," instructs the guard who escorted me. Three metal chairs occupy the room, two of which are on one side of a stainless steel desk. Trembling legs manage to lower my body down into the seat opposite the two empty chairs. My blue eyes are fixed on the concrete wall ahead, fighting for steadiness. In the eerie quiet of the room my rapidly increasing pulse makes a dull thudding sound in my ears. I hear footsteps in the hall grow louder, closer. Suddenly, the door to the room slams shut. I know an individual has just entered, but I don't dare turn my head. Every subtle signal I send with my body, no matter how innocent, will be seen, magnified, and taken into account.

Out of the corner of my eye I notice the guard is still present, standing off to the side. I lower my gaze as someone settles into the chair directly facing me. I am refusing to make eye contact as a sign of respect, but I feel the individual's eyes boring into my skull. I raise my head slightly, and for the third time in a row I find myself facing a female officer. *Have mercy on me, sister,* I pray.

"Why do you want this child?" The unexpected directness of her question catches me off guard, and her words hang frozen in the air.

No job interview has prepared me for a more loaded question. I want to wipe my sweaty palms on my pants, but instead I concentrate on what I need to say. I desperately try to recall all that I had rehearsed two days ago in the restaurant.

"I met Mark through my work at an orphanage. He was very sick. I spent a lot of time with him trying to get him to eat, to help him gain weight so that he would survive, even though the doctor said this was not possible. And over time he became really attached to me, and I to him. He was found all alone, in a latrine. I believe I am the closest thing Mark has to a family, and I would like to make our relationship more permanent. I would like to adopt him."

"All right. Now I have some further questions for you. We would not want Mark to fall into the wrong hands now, would we?" she says, without a trace of emotion in her voice.

I respectfully divert my eyes from her penetrating gaze and instead stare at her arms crossed authoritatively over her chest. Her body language offers no indication that she has an ounce of sympathy for me. *I am not the wrong hands!* I want to cry out. *I am not going to sell him on the black market. You can trust me.* I pray these exact thoughts will somehow make their way into the officer's mind.

"What are you planning on doing in Canada?" she asks.

"I have just completed my bachelor of arts degree in psychology," I explain. "I want to work in the field of social work. My interest in that field is what brought me to Uganda, to volunteer at a children's home."

"And how long do you intend to stay there?"

I've been expecting this question and have gone back and forth with how I should answer. I really want to return to Canada for one whole year, but Peter advised me to ask for only a one-month visa, telling me that once I arrived in Canada I could apply to have the visa extended to six months. But even six months seems short. It is going to take time for Mark to get settled and adjust to his new surroundings. Six months will mean that just as we begin to establish a routine, we will have to prepare to leave again. And then there is my work. Who will want to hire me knowing I have to return to Uganda in six months? Most important of all is the paperwork I have to complete so that we are on track for the adoption to be approved in Canada after the mandatory three-year foster process. I won't be able to do anything in one month, and six months will barely allow me to begin. Neither is ideal, but obviously six months is way better than one. But do I dare ask this of them? Especially considering Peter's warning that I should not expect more than one?

"One month," I reply, my voice barely above a whisper.

"How can you guarantee that you will come back?"

I open my folder containing my letters of support and copies of all of my paperwork up to this point. I made sure to include them in my application as well, but perhaps the officer didn't go over them all. I lift the first document off the pile and lay it on the desk.

"I will come back," I say, trying to exude a humble confidence. "I will come back like this letter attests."

The officer skims the letter signed by Margaret Lugawa, the orphanage director. I then hand her the letter signed by the judge in Jinja. My face is uncomfortably warm, probably covered in stress-induced red blotches.

"You can go now. Go and sit in the waiting room." Again, she speaks in a voice devoid of emotion, a skill she has perfected after hundreds of hours of questioning in rooms such as this. It is her job to remain impartial while she gathers all of her information, and she does this well, for I have absolutely no idea whether she will grant my request or not.

The guard who has been standing impossibly still makes his way toward me and indicates I am to leave with him. I gradually rise from my seat, steadying myself with one arm on the chair while the other gathers my folder to my chest, the folder that contains papers worth more to me than all the jewels in the world. I follow the guard back into the waiting room, legs wobbling as though I have had too much to drink. I am hardly able to stand under the pressure of the situation.

It's over. You did all you could do and now it is over. I think I may throw up. I distract myself by thinking of Mark, of how he now squeals when I tickle him and how he sleeps with his little ankles crossed. I try to focus on how he rubs his eyes when he wakes up in the morning, and how he loves to grab my braids and put them in his mouth.

Have faith. Believe in the impossible.

"Tandela Swann." Once again a loud male voice blurts my name through a speaker fastened to the wall above me. I am beckoned through a door that reveals a large room divided into many cubicles. Cubicles where dreams are granted or diminished. A man about thirty-five years old motions me toward his station. My interrogator stands beside him. I lower my head and stare at her hands. Her cuticles are perfectly pushed down and her nails are trimmed just below her fingertips. In what feels like slow motion, she places a piece of paper into my trembling, pale hands.

"You've got six months. That's it."

MY TRIP BACK to Jinja is thankfully without incident, and I am miraculously not faced with any difficulties when our bus crosses the border back into Uganda.

I can hardly believe that Mark and I leave Uganda in five days. I sing softly to Mark as I place him in the baby carrier and swing it over my back while he claps his hands with excitement. Mark is always content to sit in the carrier because he enjoys the rhythmic bounce of my step and his ability to view the world from a new height. Outside our little home, I take a deep breath, trying to commit to memory the scent of fragrant flowers mixed in with smoke from outdoor kitchens. I will miss Jinja. But I will be back before I know it. Six months at home is going to fly by.

"Where is Mama Teresa?" I ask Margaret during breakfast. Teresa is one of the housemothers that helps me feed the highest-needs babies.

"You haven't heard?" replies Margaret.

"Heard what?"

"Teresa, she is Acholi from the Pader district," Margaret reminds me.

A number of the housemothers here have Acholi roots tracing back to a people group who came to northern Uganda from southern Sudan. The Acholi people continue to live in northern Uganda, and Teresa, who has moved here to work, sends her earnings home to her family. She has become increasingly worried about them because villages in northern Uganda are regularly being targeted by the LRA.

In 1996, the government issued what they called a "forced displacement policy" for the district of Gulu, where the LRA has conducted more killings, rapes, and abductions than any other. Inhabitants in nearby districts — such as Pader, where Teresa is from — have been encouraged to leave their homes and relocate to displacement camps, but many are resisting because in many camps the quality of life is very low. Humanitarian agencies such as the World Food Programme support the camps with supplies; however, they are repeatedly ambushed and robbed en route, leaving the camps with very little food. And so the Acholi people are left with few options — risk their lives by staying where they are, or go to displacement camps. Neither promises that they will live.

"Last night she got news that the LRA had attacked her village," Margaret continues. "No one from the village has been heard from, so it is unlikely that any of Teresa's family are still alive." Margaret sighs a sigh I have come to know well, a sigh that means tragedy is weighing heavily on her mind. "We will never know how many children were stolen." I don't have to ask what the soldiers will do with the children. I have overheard enough conversations to know of the horrors that await them. The young girls will be forced to take on the domestic duties for the LRA commanders and at the age of twelve or thirteen will be raped and taken as wives, thus putting them at risk for sexually transmitted diseases and forcing them to give birth to children in remote areas with no medical care.

The young boys will be brainwashed and forced to be child soldiers. A common brainwashing technique used by the LRA is singling out a boy who may be too weak to be an asset, then beating him to death in front of his peers, thereby instilling the fear in everyone else that a similar fate awaits all who disobey orders or try to escape. Another common tactic is to hold a gun to the head of a young boy while forcing him to kill his friend or his brother. Often these atrocities are committed in places so far removed from towns or villages that the children know if they do manage to escape they will most likely starve to death while searching for help. Returning to one's family is often not an option; either one's entire village has been destroyed or any surviving family members will have scattered to take refuge in unknown areas.

The conflict in northern Uganda is getting worse every day, and it is now estimated that over half a million people are taking refuge in displacement camps. I saw a photo on the news of a man who had been mutilated and was receiving treatment in a Kampala hospital. His nose had been cut off, leaving two giant holes where his nostrils were and only a thin layer of skin in between to keep them separated. His hands had also been cut off.

"I do not know when she will be coming back." Margaret's long arm reaches for a sippy cup that has fallen to the floor. She patiently places it between the little hands that flung it down. Keeping composed, as she always does when faced with upsetting news, she wipes her hands on the dishrag that hangs from her waist.

I spoon some porridge into the mouth of the baby sitting on my left, then pat Mark's knee with my other hand as he lifts his sippy cup to his lips, finishing the last of his breakfast.

Struggling to process the reality of Teresa's situation, I ask Margaret how she deals with such news and the fact that such horrific acts go largely unnoticed by the rest of the world. "We are so quick to condemn mass genocides in history and yet turn a blind eye to the ones going on in the present," I utter in disbelief.

"We can't let the LRA defeat us, or them." With firm resolve Margaret gestures to the scene around us, a room full of life with the plethora of jubilant little children enjoying the last of their millet, the air a mixture of giggles and cries. She continues to share that the job of the housemothers here is hard enough; if they were to allow themselves to be shattered every time they learned how the LRA ruined someone's life, they would never have the strength to attend to all the children who have been entrusted into their care, children who may be blessed to grow up unscathed by this war. Margaret points out that before I came here, I had no idea of how people's lives were being affected by the LRA, and now I have witnessed the war's bloodshed firsthand. And I will not forget what I have seen and heard.

But now that I know about the war, what do I do? When I go home to Canada, my daily life will be far removed from it. I will not have to worry about arriving at work and hearing another gut-wrenching story about how my friend's family was murdered, or her children kidnapped, or her sister raped and left for dead. No, I will not, but someone else will. Time and time again. These are real stories, and they need to be shared.

My eyes rest on Mark who is gazing with wide-eyed delight at all the action around him, flinging porridge into the air as he claps his hands. Though his life has been much different from that of a child solider, I am mindful that he has his own story that must be shared with him one day. When he is old enough to understand, I look forward to telling him about how God brought us together and all that we did together here in Jinja. I will speak often of our friends here, for I long for him to know the character and culture of the people of his birth country and the complex history that surrounds Uganda. I don't know how much more of Mark's life will be spent in Uganda, and I want him to treasure the truth that God had a very special reason for beginning his life here.

CHAPTER NINE

March–May 2004, Canada

M ARCH **8TH** has finally arrived.

Our trip home to Calgary is uneventful, but absolutely exhausting nonetheless. Traveling alone with an infant means that I am constantly thinking about the logistics of what Mark needs: where I can get ahold of appropriate food for him, where I can change his diaper, how to get us both through security, and figuring out where our gate is located. Then, once we are on the plane, I have to squeeze the baby carrier into the overhead compartment while making sure we have everything we need for the flight tucked below our seat. Once that is taken care of, I begin to try to occupy Mark for the duration of the flight—or until he falls asleep—so that he doesn't get overly antsy.

Our first flight is from Kampala to Dubai. We land in Dubai late at night, and since our next flight departs early in the morning, we spend the night at the airport. Mark lies in my lap, attempting to sleep. We then make our way to Paris, and from Paris to Toronto. On this leg of the trip we are blessed to secure a seat equipped with a baby cot that enables Mark to sleep comfortably for a few hours. This is my first travel experience with a baby, and I get the impression from other travelers that Mark is unusually easygoing. Even though he must be incredibly tired, Mark rarely cries. On every flight, fellow passengers ask to hold him and play with him, giving my arms a break and helping to pass the time.

When we arrive in Toronto it is two o'clock in the afternoon. All I want to do is crawl into a bed and sleep for the next week. What gives me a little spurt of energy is knowing that I am going to introduce Mark to a longtime friend. Brianne, my roommate from university, lives in Toronto and is coming to the airport to see us during our layover. Brianne is waiting for us in the arrivals area right outside customs. But before we can walk through those doors, we first have to get through Canada Customs and Immigration. Despite the fact that there is snow on the ground outside, I begin to perspire, apprehensive of how Mark's visa will be received.

"He has a six-month visa," the immigration officer states as he scans our passports.

"Yes," I reply.

I haven't anticipated there will be a problem, but after all the difficulties I've had with authority figures in Uganda, watching the customs officer go through our passports causes the hairs on my forearms to stand on end.

"And who is he to you?"

In the carrier behind me, Mark's hand gently tugs on my braids. At the warmth of his little hand my nerves abruptly subside and are replaced with joy. A self-assured smile broadens my face as I ponder the remarkable truth of who Mark is to me. "I am fostering him and I plan on adopting him."

"Do you want to stay in Canada for only six months?" The officer's serious eyes search my face, curious to know my answer.

"No, I would like to stay longer," I answer honestly, surprised at the question.

"Well, how much longer do you want?"

Did I hear him correctly? Is this his way of offering us more time in Canada? If I could get just six more months to work on the Canadian adoption criteria here that would be amazing.

"How about a year?" I venture.

"Fine."

Thump. Thump. He stamps our two passports. In a matter of seconds, Mark's visa has gone from six months to a year. *Thank you, Jesus.* I hurry out of the immigration area before the officer can change his mind, Mark bouncing on my back in the baby carrier with each step I take.

"Tandy!" a voice cries out.

Brianne has more energy than anyone else I know, and her smile, always infectious, is even brighter than usual. It is familiar. She wraps her arms around both of us in a hug.

"How are you? Hi, Mark! Oh, Tandy, I can't believe this little guy is your son! Hi, honey," she places her finger in Mark's fist. "Can I take him out?" she asks, gesturing to the carrier.

"Go for it." I turn my back toward her.

"He'll be okay with me?"

"He's spent the first year of his life in an orphanage being passed around from one housemother to the next," I explain. "And on our last flight, when he wasn't sleeping, he was passed up and down the aisle. Everyone wanted to hold him. He'll be fine."

"This still feels surreal," Brianne says. "I remember exactly where I was when I got your email explaining that you were taking Mark in as a foster child and were planning on adopting him. I was in Smugglers Cove, Vermont, with the team." Brianne is a coach with the national Paralympic ski team. "That was back in December. And I was thinking, *Oh my gosh, Tandy is going to be a mom.* And here you are!"

Brianne bounces Mark up and down in her lap, her index fingers tightly grasped in each of his fists. It is as though they are old friends, the way Mark giggles uncontrollably every time she laughs. I comment that Mark's hair has grown a lot recently, and gently pat the thick, coarse black spirals that cover his head. Only a year ago Brianne and I were living together and talking about our plans for the future, a stark reminder that though we may make plans, only God knows what is truly in store for each of us. The whites of Mark's four front teeth shine against his dark skin when he smiles, a sight that never fails to fill me with bliss, and I know that God's plan has far surpassed my own greatest aspirations, even though our future is still largely unknown.

I notice that almost everyone who passes by can't help but let their eyes linger on Mark and Brianne. During our two-hour visit, more than a dozen people stop to comment on how cute Mark is. I know Mark is cute, but it's more than his cuteness that elicits glances from strangers. It is because Mark stands out. This is an acute reminder that we are not in Uganda anymore and little black babies are not a common sight, especially when held by a young white woman. During our international flights, there was always a number of people of African descent around us in the airport and on our flights. But I know there is a strong likelihood that on our flight to Calgary Mark will be the only black person, something that will make us stand out more than we already do.

This presumption proves to be true, yet I am so fatigued that I barely notice how we catch everyone's eye as we walk down the aisle to our seats. My time with Brianne distracted me from how tired I was, and I can barely lift my arms over my head to place the baby carrier in the overhead compartment. This flight is scheduled to be less than four hours long, which is short in comparison to all our other flights so far, but the minutes tick by far slower as I slump in my seat, Mark sprawled out with his back resting on my tummy, his hands clutching the teddy bear that he sleeps with every night.

Tears of relief begin to stream down my cheeks as soon as we step through the arrival doors at the Calgary International Airport. I can finally let go. *We made it.* There are no more barriers preventing us from coming home. I see my family—Mom, Dad, Nathan, Kirsten, and Kirsten's husband, Kelly—huddled close together, waiting for us. My steps quicken, and as I get closer I can tell that they are all crying, too. Kirsten in particular is shaking with emotion. Two weeks ago, Kirsten told me that she was eight weeks pregnant with her and Kelly's first child. I cried over the phone with the news that Mark was going to have a cousin close to his own age.

I collapse into Mom's embrace, allowing the strength of her arms to hold me up. I lean into her, cherishing the emotional support that emanates from her touch. She squeezes me tightly, letting go only out of her excitement to meet Mark. I take the baby carrier off my back and lift Mark out.

"I just want to hug him and never let him go, but I don't want to overwhelm him," Mom confesses, stretching out her arms to hold Mark for the very first time.

Kirsten steps toward me. Overcome with emotion, she cannot speak. Our cheeks touch and our tears mingle as she wraps her arms around me. I feel her body slacken, as though she can finally relax, knowing that Mark and I have come home at long last.

"I thought he was much bigger," Dad comments, taking Mark's hand in his.

"Yes, in the picture you sent us Mark looked bigger than he does now," Mom echoes. "Oh, Tandy, I am so proud of you, honey."

"I still remember the day you left for Uganda. And now you have come back a mother," Kirsten says with awe, unable to take her eyes off Mark.

Mom kisses him on the top of his head. "You are just a miracle. He has no signs of kwashiorkor," she continues, referring to a protein deficiency common in children who have suffered malnutrition, which manifests as a swollen belly, whitish tinge to the hair, shiny skin, and weak teeth.

"He had a little pot belly when I first met him," I reply, thinking back to what Mark looked like when I hardly knew him at all.

"It must be because you took him in so early," Mom concludes. "He looks amazing. I can't believe how well he has developed considering his birth history and all the infections and illnesses he suffered when he was so little."

Although Mark has gained substantial weight over the last two months, he is still considered small for his age. No one comments on how I look, other than my hair being a mass of tiny braids. I know I've gained weight. The extra ten pounds are a physical reminder of the high-starch Ugandan diet I have been eating for the last six months.

"I couldn't sleep at all last night, Tandy," Kirsten shares as we make our way to the parking lot. "On the one hand I was ecstatic that I was finally going to see you and meet Mark, and on the other hand I couldn't shake the feeling that something was going to happen to prevent you from arriving, that this was too good to be true. So I kept praying. It was like the night before my wedding day. I could hardly wait and couldn't quite believe it was for real."

TWO DAYS LATER, we celebrate Mark's birthday. In all the photos we take, he looks stunned. This is to be expected, I guess, considering it is only his second day in

Canada. Do any one-year-olds have any idea of what is going on at their birthday, anyway? Not to mention the added ridiculousness of the dorky party hats situated on everyone's heads.

We sing "Happy Birthday" to Mark as he stares at the chocolate cake before him. One large candle burns in the middle.

"Let's blow out the candle," I whisper, leaning forward over his shoulder toward the cake.

I have been dreaming of this moment. Today is March 11th, 2004, and my entire family, all seven of us, are seated around the chestnut dining table at Mom and Dad's. The table, usually covered in papers or one of Mom's arts and crafts projects, has been cleared for the celebration. Shelves stacked to the ceiling with books line one end of the room while a piano sits under the window that faces the park across the street. Mark stares wide-eyed at his cake, playing with his hands.

"He must be a bit shell-shocked," Kirsten comments. "There is so much to process, so much happening all at once."

I agree. He is unusually quiet, taking it all in.

After our birthday festivities, I take him into the bedroom that we are sharing. I change his diaper and select one of the many pairs of pajamas that I find in the dresser. In her expectant-grandma excitement, Mom has stocked the house with clothes and toys for Mark, many of which she got from friends and family who were all too happy to contribute.

I sit in a rocking chair in a corner of the room, moving gently while Mark begins to fall asleep. My lashes dampen as I gaze down at him. This past week has been full of competing emotions. It is difficult to believe all that has transpired since I left for Uganda six months ago. The life I lived before I got on that plane for Kampala has, in a sense, ended. Now Mark is here. Home. He was found in the bottom of an outhouse twelve months ago, and by God's grace, has now just celebrated his first birthday with people that will hopefully be his family forever. As Mark closes his eyes, I give thanks to God for making this homecoming possible.

Carefully shutting the door to our room behind me, I join Kirsten on the couch.

"Does it come naturally?" she asks, looking down at her hands resting on her tummy. "Being a mom?"

"I think so." I pause. "I feel like I don't know what I am doing half the time, but yes, it feels more natural, more intuitive, than I ever would have thought. You are going to be a great mom." I flash her a reassuring smile. "You've always been way more maternal than me."

"Mom used to have to remind me that you didn't need two moms." We both burst out laughing then quickly quiet each other down. "I have always felt very protective of you," she whispers. Kirsten is smiling, yet her brow tightens and I can see there is sadness in her eyes. "I wish I could have been there with you," she confesses. "I feel like I've already missed so much. Like twins who are used to experiencing everything together, and then they get separated. While they are separated, one of the twins has this amazing, life-changing experience, and even though she shares as many details as she can, the other twin knows she has missed something very significant. I can't help but feel this sadness because I've missed witnessing you become a mother." She rubs one hand over her belly and gently touches my knee with the other.

"You're a mom now," she repeats to herself. "It still doesn't feel real sometimes. Do you remember when we were little and Mom and Dad would take us to the ski hill? I would sit in the hut and cry for what felt like hours before I got the nerve to go down the bunny hill, while you went down right away. As a young child, you always had this mentality that you could tackle anything. Things don't scare you like they scare me."

"But I do get scared. And this thing with Mark, it's not about being brave. You know that feeling you had when you learned you were pregnant? How you immediately loved the little baby inside you, even though he or she is smaller than a nut?"

"Yeah. There is this little life, with a future in store, which I am carrying within me. Part of Kelly, part of me." She gazes downward, her body as fit and lean as ever, months away from revealing a significant baby bump.

"It's hard to explain, right? The intense love and protection you feel for this baby that you haven't yet met face to face? This is how I feel about Mark. It wasn't because he was dying that I began to care for him so much. His poor health was just one way that God drew us together. I can't explain how one day I became his mother, it just happened."

I share with Kirsten how I've continued to grow into being a mother as Mark himself has grown. I reassure her that it's okay to feel barely capable, if not completely incapable, of the weighty responsibility of raising a child. "But day by day, God will grow you and strengthen you and build you into exactly the mother you need to be for this baby, one day at a time. One thing I've learned over the last couple of months is only God knows what the future will bring, and thank God he does, because in his own perfect way he begins to prepare us for it long in advance."

LATER IN MAY, I move to my old room upstairs, giving Mark and me separate sleeping quarters. The change is supposed to help me get more sleep, but I'm not sure if I'll get much sleep tonight. Tomorrow Mark and I have an appointment at the Infectious Disease Clinic at Alberta Children's Hospital. For what feels like the hundredth time today, I pray Mark will not test positive for HIV. In Uganda, approximately twenty-five percent of orphans have been orphaned as a result of the AIDS epidemic. If Mark's birth mother had the virus, it is likely that Mark contracted it when he was born. There was the option to have Mark tested in Uganda, but I decided against it because a positive result would have disqualified Mark from being an eligible foster child.

Because of the trauma and suffering Mark endured as a newborn, I have come to terms with the fact he may be sickly or have acute special needs for the rest of his life. From the moment I began to contemplate fostering him, I have been preparing myself for the reality that Mark is HIV-positive or has some other future diagnosis that will affect him for the rest of his life.

I can't help but wonder, *Is a healthy child the be-all and end-all? Are we not all created by God, exactly as we ought to be, healthy or otherwise?* If I really believe that God creates everyone with inerrant precision, I have to surrender Mark's health completely and accept with faith whatever prognosis we are handed. Children that have special needs are not defective, for God does not make mistakes. He chooses the who, the how, and the why. I may share the same genes as my parents, but this does not mean God played a greater role in creating me to be their daughter than he did in creating Mark to be my son. Mark is not a possession that I own; he is a gift from God that I am to steward as best I can with God's guidance, in sickness and in health.

I reach for the Bible beside my bed and turn to the beginning of the Gospel of Luke where Mary is still trying to process what the angel Gabriel told her, that she will conceive in her womb a son named Jesus who will be called holy—the Son of God. As I read this passage, my spirit is encouraged. God has given Mary very little knowledge of what he has in store for her and for this little baby that she will bear. Not worn down by the unknown, nor overcome by fear, Mary proclaims:

> My soul glorifies the Lord
>   and my spirit rejoices in God my Savior,
> for he has been mindful
>   of the humble state of his servant.
> From now on all generations will call me blessed,
>   for the Mighty One has done great things
>   for me —
>   holy is his name.
> His mercy extends to those who fear him,
>   from generation to generation.
>
> *(Luke 1:46-50)*

I have the same God. This same God has shown me his might over the last few months in the great things he has done for Mark and me. I pray for a faith like Mary's. I pray that no matter what the results of the tests reveal, I will believe God is good, sovereign, and powerful. He is able to fill me with joy no matter what circumstances I face.

"IT USED TO be very difficult for us to detect HIV in an infant," the nurse conducting the test explains.

Mom has come with Mark and me on this crisp and bright May morning, for which I am very thankful. I remember how upset Mark was in Uganda when he had to receive an IV, and the test today requires a blood sample. I am praying that the incident in Uganda was a one-time thing.

As the nurse skims through Mark's paperwork, she tells us that scientists have now developed accurate blood tests for infants as young as six months. She glances up from the papers and adds that there has been incredible progress in the area of HIV research.

"You can live with HIV now with these amazing antiretroviral drugs they have developed," she says, pushing Mark's forms to one side of the desk. "Now, if I can just get him to sit still on your lap. Is he allergic to latex?"

"No. He has no allergies that we're aware of." I gently wrap my arms around him, trying to make him feel as secure as possible under the circumstances.

"Mark, here is your teddy," says Mom. Mark reaches out and grabs the precious teddy bear he was given as an infant at the orphanage. It is the one thing he has to have to fall asleep. He holds it fiercely to his chest.

"Can you hold this ball in your fist, Mark?" asks the nurse gently. She hands him a sparkly ball. If he can keep his fist closed it will cause the veins to plump up a bit.

"That is a nice teddy," the nurse says as she swiftly ties a rubber band below his elbow to constrict the blood flow. "Does it have a name?"

She continues talking to Mark as she feels around his arm for a vein. I can soon tell she is having the same problem that the nurses at the Jinja hospital encountered. Being a baby, his veins are already very small, and his dark skin makes them even harder to find.

"It was really challenging in Uganda for the nurses to find a vein when Mark needed an IV. We ended up using a butterfly needle in the back of his hand where the veins were bigger."

"Yes, I think that is what we are going to have to do here, too." The nurse unties the tourniquet on Mark's forearm and picks up a cotton swab from the counter. She soaks it in alcohol and then rubs the area on his hand where she will insert the needle.

"And you are so lucky that your Nana is here today with you, too," she says to Mark as she attempts to quickly insert the needle. But just at the last instant, Mark flinches. And she misses. His forehead smacks my nose as he twists away from the nurse in horror. I try to quickly regain my focus, shaking my head to get rid of the spots in my vision as Mark sobs into my chest.

"Mark, this is going to be okay. We just have to let the nurse do this and it will be over really quickly. You just sit here in my lap, sweetie; I will hold your hand." But Mark is having none of this. Instead, his screams get louder and louder.

"Here, let me help," says my mom, picking his teddy bear off the floor. "Mark, can you hold your teddy? I think your teddy needs you," she says as she tries to hold Mark's flailing arm still enough for the nurse to make another attempt.

Mark spies the needle and begins to kick violently. He is too young to understand what the nurse is trying to do, and all he knows is that this person has been prodding his skin and he wants nothing to do with her. I force myself to draw deep breaths, trying to stem my tears. It breaks my heart to hear his pain and see how scared he is. The nurse leaves and returns ten minutes later with a colleague. As soon as Mark sees her, he starts screaming again.

"Laura here is really good at finding challenging veins," she says. Laura lives up to her reputation and inserts the needle with relative ease while the three of us manage to hold Mark down.

"Here, Mark, what do you think of these stickers?" the first nurse says once the last vial of blood has been taken. Mark turns his tear-streaked face toward her and is immediately distracted by the animal stickers that the nurse has stuck on his shirt.

"He's being tested for HIV, syphilis, and a number of skin disorders to see if his dry skin is related. I see on the referral from your doctor that the lab is going to do a lot of additional tests, even though Mark doesn't seem to have visible symptoms for any of them. I guess your doctor just wants to be sure. Might as well; you don't want to have to go through this again. We'll see you back here in two days for the results." She smiles reassuringly.

LATER THAT DAY, Nathan comes over to visit Mark. Nathan has moved out, but ever since Mark and I have been here he comes over fairly regularly. Mark is bouncing up and down in his car-shaped Exersaucer. When he sees Nathan approach, he reaches out his arm and makes a fist with his hand. Nathan does the same, and they pound their fists together. Mark arcs his back with glee, for he finds "doing the pound," as we call it, hilarious. Nathan turns on some hip-hop music.

"Look, Tandy, he's bouncing with the beat!" Sure

enough, Mark's little body is going up and down in time with the music.

"Maybe it's because Dad's been playing the guitar for him so much," I say. Mark loves to sit next to my dad on the couch while Dad sings and plays his guitar.

"Come here, big guy." Nathan lifts Mark out of the Exersaucer and lays him on his back. Mark giggles with glee as Nathan tickles him.

"So I hear you got a job?" Nathan asks me.

"Yes," I reply. "At the Salvation Army. I start the first week of June."

I've been home for over two months now and felt it was time that I get a job so I could begin putting some money aside for Mark and me. I had worked at a Salvation Army shelter downtown the summer before my last year of university and made contact with them a month ago to see if they had any positions available. They offered me a job working the night shift at the shelter. The job is going to be challenging emotionally, for I will constantly be in contact with people who are living in very difficult circumstances. However, I really wanted a job where I will be working face to face with people and trying to help them in some way, so I was happy to accept the position.

"Are you looking forward to it?" he asks.

"I need a job. I can't live off Mom and Dad forever," I confess. "It'll be okay for now."

"So what will happen with Mark?" Nathan asks. "Are you doing daycare?"

"Mom's going to help me."

My work hours will be from eleven at night to seven in the morning. I will be with Mark in the morning, and then when Mom is home in the afternoon from her work as a physician at a geriatric clinic, she will look after Mark and let me get some sleep before my shift starts. I have struggled on and off with insomnia for years, so I am used to living on little sleep. Because Mark is a fairly calm child, content to play in one place for quite a long time, I think I'll be able to manage being on my own with him after my shift until Mom can take over and let me rest.

"You think that will work out okay? I can help, too, whenever you need it," Nathan says, turning his attention to Mark. "Do we have fun together?" He throws Mark in the air and Mark squeals with delight. "Do you have fun with your silly Uncle Nathan?"

I can't remember the last time I saw Nathan cheerful and relaxed. I've noticed that whenever he is around Mark, Nathan's eyes light up, giving me a glimpse of his old self. It is as though something about Mark's presence frees Nathan to be happy again.

The following afternoon, Nathan takes Mark to the park across the street while Mom and I stay back to cook dinner. After the lasagna is in the oven, Mom makes us a cup of tea.

"He's changed Nathan," Mom observes, nodding in the direction of the park. She exhales a heavy sigh of relief, yet I still detect a slight hint of worry in her eyes.

"Mark has?" I ask.

"Yes. You know how depressed Nathan was before you left. Well, there was no change while you were gone, and perhaps things even got worse. It has been so hard on him, Tandy, losing his friends like he did. He felt that there was no joy left in his life and nothing left to live for. Everything was broken.

"But in the last two months, since he met Mark, he has slowly begun to change. It is as though Mark has given him a reason for living," Mom explains. She goes on to remind me that she has been praying that God would bring a man into Nathan's life who could act as a mentor to him and come alongside him during this difficult time. "I think that prayer has been answered in Mark," she shares. "He is the one God has sent to help

Nathan break through this. God has used Mark to give Nathan hope again."

"It's true."

Our heads swivel toward the door where Nathan is standing. I didn't even hear him and Mark come in.

"How can I be mad at the world when I'm around Mark? Mark is the only one who doesn't know my past. He doesn't deserve to have a grumpy uncle; it's not his fault that I have baggage. Mark lifts my spirits and reminds me that life isn't pointless."

My mom turns her head back toward me as she wipes a tear from her eye. At long last she is seeing how her prayers have come to fruition. It wasn't in the form of a wise, well-educated, and successful grown man, but rather a toddler from Uganda. Nathan swings Mark over his shoulder like a sack of potatoes and they head to the living room in search of some toys.

The sight of the two of them together brings me such joy, yet at the same time makes my heart ache for a daddy for Mark.

I remember when Mark first said "dada." It was not long after he had taken his first steps. Kirsten and Kelly were over and we were all cheering Mark on, coaxing him to practise walking toward us. Mark plunked himself down on the carpet and, out of the blue, said "dada." It got really quiet. "Dada," he said again, clapping his hands.

"Tandy, it doesn't mean anything," Mom quickly tried to reassure me. "It's just a really easy thing to say. He doesn't even know what it means." But her words didn't take away the feeling inside of me. Those two syllables pierced my heart.

Later on that evening I whispered in his ear, "I want you to have a daddy, too. More than anything. I am sorry that all I can offer you is me." Ever since that day, in our bedtime prayers, we have asked God to bring Mark a daddy.

TWO DAYS AFTER the test was conducted, we return to the Infectious Disease Clinic. I have tried to mentally prepare myself for the result that Mark is HIV-positive by spending hours on the computer last night reading about antiretroviral therapies, and how early treatment can help prevent HIV damaging the immune system. I'm thankful that we still have nine months here before we have to go back to Uganda, and plenty of time to get Mark's medication routine established. Mark is playing on the floor with two trucks when a doctor breezes in.

"Well, you've got nothing to worry about; he is perfectly healthy," he proclaims.

My legs stagger forward, and I stretch out my arm to steady myself on the chair in front of me. My fingers clutch at the hard plastic of the chair, my body too stunned to move. The shock of the news has stalled my breathing, and I am left moving my lips but unable to speak. I reach for Mark's hand, treasuring his warm touch. I know for certain that no test result in the world could alter my devotion to Mark, my precious little gift from God. After being left to die on the day he was born, suffering numerous infections in his first year of life, and being labeled the weakest and most sickly of all the babies at the orphanage, Mark has been given a clean bill of health. God, for his good purpose and plan, has now miraculously intervened to bless Mark with a beautifully healthy body.

CHAPTER TEN

June 2004–February 2006, Canada

O NCE I start work at the Salvation Army, the days
begin to fly by. The late summer and fall months are
a very exciting time, particularly with Kirsten giving
birth to Koen in September. Mom and Dad are blessed
to now have two grandsons. Mark and I start to attend
a church with a large African community. I want him
to have some people in his life that share both his skin
colour and the culture of his birth country.

Sharon and I continue to keep in touch through
email, and she recently began her university studies

in Kampala after receiving news this summer that she was awarded a scholarship. She still manages to visit the orphanage once or twice a month, so she has kept me up to date on how everyone is doing. They have received a few more babies, and have also secured placements for some of the older children at an orphanage in Kampala that is able to provide their children with full-time schooling. Margaret is still there, working hard and running a tight ship. Solomon has fully recovered from his accident and is back at his post at the main gate.

Though life is busy and full of good things, I sense the night shifts at the Salvation Army taking their toll on me. Not only are the hours hard on my body, the work itself is very intense. There are so many hurting, broken people that come through our doors needing more help than we can give. I spend most of my time feeling very inadequate. I want to do more; I want to be able to address the root of the circumstances that bring people into our shelter. But this is an objective way beyond my means.

I know I am close to burning out.

Recognizing the signs, I begin looking for a new job that allows me to sleep at night. I am offered a position with Catholic Family Services in which I am responsible for overseeing a program for teen moms. Kirsten has offered to look after Mark during the day. But at first I am hesitant to accept her offer.

"Kir, you have a newborn. Adding a one-and-a-half-year-old will be asking too much."

"No, it'll be okay. Mark is so good. He's unlike any baby I have ever known."

I can't help but agree with my sister. Mark is extremely easygoing and unusually obedient for his age. I can pretty much take him anywhere without having to worry about him making a scene. If I meet a friend for lunch, Mark will sit in a high chair or his stroller and eat his food and smile at everyone walking by. Strangers comment that he is the best-behaved baby they have ever seen. Mark rarely cries, and when he does it is because he is really hungry or tired. I have also noticed that Mark does not need to be constantly entertained like most one-year-olds. Instead, he is content to play with his blocks or his Fisher-Price stacking rings for over an hour on the floor.

"I don't know if his good behaviour stems from his natural disposition alone or if it's also related to the first months of his life," I confide to Kirsten. "I wonder if the unusual circumstances surrounding his birth play a part in him wanting to please me. Maybe he's so compliant because unconsciously he's still worried about being accepted."

Or perhaps he is so good because God knew that was all I could handle. Still, I am nervous about Kirsten having Mark and Koen all day by herself. On the first day, after my shift ends at four o'clock, I rush over to her place to relieve her.

"You wouldn't believe what he did today," Kirsten says when I arrive. "I laid Koen down in his reclining chair while I was making lunch," she begins. "And I look over and Mark gets up from his blocks and walks over to Koen, and then sits down beside him. He sits quietly beside him the whole time I am making lunch. Koen can't even do anything yet, he doesn't even move hardly, and Mark just sat there, as though he wanted to protect Koen and keep him company."

As the months go by, Kirsten shares more stories about Mark's relationship with his baby cousin. When Koen becomes more interactive, Mark starts to bring him toys. When Koen begins to teethe, Mark lets him chew on his fingers. Even though Mark can walk, he prefers to squat or lie down when he is around Koen so that they can look at each other. As the bond between the cousins grows, Mark's character traits become more and more apparent. He takes great satisfaction in helping settle Koen when he is upset, and is most content himself when reassured that everyone around him is happy. With strangers and in public settings, Mark continues to be quiet. However, when at home with his family, he blossoms into a boisterous and self-confident toddler. At only twenty months, he has proved to be extremely coordinated, convincing his proud Uncle Nathan that he shows great athletic promise.

WELL AWARE THAT Mark's initial extended visa expires in March 2005, I begin researching the Canadian adoption requirements. I learn we need to undergo a home assessment and have criminal record checks done on me as well as my parents since Mark and I are living with them. However, it is important these two requirements be completed in close proximity to our court date in Uganda, for they need to be as up to date as possible. I still have to foster Mark for two more years until Uganda will consider my adoption request. If I spend these two years in Uganda, it will be nearly impossible to satisfy the Canadian adoption require-ments; therefore, my only hope lies in getting Mark's Canadian visa extended.

In January of 2005, I decide to apply for a one-year extension on Mark's visa. I receive a letter in February informing me that an interview has been scheduled for me at the Citizenship and Immigration Canada office in downtown Calgary on February 23rd. I am required to bring the following original documents for inspection:

- Any documents and correspondence regarding Mark's foster care;
- Any recent correspondence from Uganda regarding the adoption/foster care;
- Any information in regard to adoption laws and procedures in Uganda;
- A valid passport for both Mark and me; and
- Proof of financial support, including bank statements from the last three months.

My appointment is at one o'clock, meaning I have to take the afternoon off work. I bring with me every document I have to date on Mark, as well as letters of correspondence between myself and Mr. Makiywe, believing these letters written to me directly from a probation officer in Uganda will add legitimacy to my plea to extend my time with Mark in Canada. I remember how relaxed the Canadian customs officer was when he asked how long I wanted Mark to stay in Canada, and am hopeful that this interview will have a similar outcome.

The officer in charge of reviewing our case looks over my documentation and asks a few clarifying questions. Then she laces her fingers together and rests her elbows on her desk.

"I cannot approve this request," she tells me. "What you have shown me here does not provide enough reassurance that the Ugandan government is aware and supportive of this request. You have one month to provide me with documentation from Ugandan authorities that this request meets with their approval. If you can't meet this requirement, you and Mark will have to leave immediately for Uganda."

My jaw slackens in disbelief at this devastating news. With trembling legs I step out of the elevator onto the main floor of the building, my mind reeling with the improbability that I can satisfy the case officer's demands. One month! Perhaps this may be possible in two months, but one? In Uganda, it was difficult enough for me to get things done in person, never mind when I am on the other side of the world.

Mr. Makiywe is the only person I can think of who may have enough authority to satisfy Canadian Immigration. He will have to sign a letter that specifically states he is supportive and knowledgeable of my request that Mark live with me in Canada for two more years. As I've done in the past, I will have to write such a letter for him. The problem is that it is too risky to mail him a letter and hope he will be punctual with its return. Not only could the letter get delayed or lost en route, but once it reaches his office it is likely to get buried in a pile of paperwork for weeks.

No, I'll have to go about this some other way. If only I could get someone reliable to go to Mr. Makiywe's office in person and have him sign the letter on the spot. But who could do this for me?

Sharon!

No one is more reliable than Sharon. It is seven-thirty in the morning in Uganda; Sharon will be awake now. I dial her number.

"Tandela, so good to hear from you!"

The sound of her voice calms me and causes me to miss her all at once.

"How are you, and how is Mark?"

"He's doing really well. I can't believe he is going to be two in just a couple of weeks. The time has gone by so fast."

Sharon quickly fills me in on how her studies are going. I know she has to catch the bus soon to get to class, and I don't want to make her late.

"Sharon, I need to get Mr. Makiywe to sign a letter proving that he is supportive of my request to the Canadian government to get another twelve-month visa for Mark. If I don't have the letter back here in thirty days, they are doing to deport me and Mark to Uganda. Can you help us with this?"

"You know I would do anything for you and Mark. Email me the letter and I will take it to his office. I promise you, I won't leave his office until it is signed. Then I'll mail it to you."

I am confident that Sharon will do everything in her power to get this document back to me quickly. She will be polite but aggressive because she knows what is at stake.

I make my own letterhead by typing the name and address of the Department of Probation and Social Welfare at the top of the page. The letter must look as official as possible. For the subject line I write, "Re: Custody of Mark by Tandela Swann." The letter reads:

The Department of Probation in Jinja District is aware that Mark is in custody with Tandela Swann in Canada awaiting adoption.

The Department of Probation in Jinja District knows that she will be returning to Uganda before the end of the third year to finish adoption papers of Mark.

Thank you very much for your attention in this matter.

N.E. Makiywe
Probation Officer

In addition to the letter, I include this note to Mr. Makiywe:

Dear Mr. Makiywe,
I have been informed by the Canadian government that in order for them to officially renew Mark's visa for another year, they require documentation from a Ugandan authority that attests that someone in Uganda is aware that Mark and I are temporarily in Canada and planning to return to Uganda to finalize the adoption process. I have not wanted to trouble you regarding this matter so have typed up a letter for you to sign should you want to help me in this matter.

Most sincerely,
Tandela Swann

I email Sharon the documents. Now all I can do is pray. And wait.

EIGHT DAYS BEFORE my documentation is due at Canadian Immigration, the letter with Mr. Makiywe's signature arrives. I am reminded of how without Sharon's help it is very unlikely I ever would have secured a birth certificate for Mark, and God has used her yet again to provide a crucial piece of documentation.

Mom decides she wants to submit a letter to the Canadian authorities as well, testifying to our family's commitment to Mark and to my plan to adopt him. Before slipping the letter into the envelope that I will personally deliver tomorrow to the Citizenship and Immigration office, I glance at it again, appreciating the reflections and insights my mother shares as she makes the argument that it would be better for both Mark and me to spend the remainder of his foster care period in Canada. In particular, she writes:

While in Uganda, for the four months that Mark was under Tandela's care, both she and Mark contracted malaria twice and Mark developed an orbital cellulitis that required a course of intravenous antibiotics. They both survived these illnesses without any significant sequelae but access to good medical services are limited in Uganda, especially for orphaned children.

Mark has already bonded to Tandela and his adopted family here in Canada. As they have been living with us, he has gotten to know us and love us as we have him. They are constantly surrounded by her family (she also has a brother, sister, brother-in-law and nephew living here in Calgary) and friends here in Calgary who offer her and Mark tremendous support.

Tandela has just acquired a better paying job with benefits and a supportive work environment for her as a single mom where there is room for advancement and professional development. If Mark is not allowed to remain in Canada she will have to quit this job in order to return with him to Uganda.

I deliver the package the next morning after dropping Mark off at Kirsten's. As soon as I get back into my car I begin to pray aloud, for it is the only thing that will keep me from collapsing in a heap of tears. *I must keep going. I can't just remove myself from the world until I hear back from them.*

Over the next week, each day passes at an agonizingly slow pace. Work-related tasks that I once considered to have great significance seem trivial as I wait with expectation to learn whether I can continue to call Canada home. Seven days after handing in the documents, I receive a letter in the mail. My shaking fingers open it with great trepidation. Mark and I are the only ones home. I wonder if I should wait for Mom or Dad. If the answer is no I'm not sure how I will cope. The response is in the first lines of the letter. Our application for a twelve-month visa has been approved.

"Mark!" I startle him with my yell. He has no idea what the letter means, no idea why Mommy's face has erupted into an enormous smile. All he knows is that Mommy looks very, very happy. Gripping the letter with one hand, I extend my other arm and give Mark the thumbs up. He grins back at me, makes a little fist, and jubilantly thrusts his thumb into the air.

Thank you, Jesus.

One year later, in February 2006, we go through a similar process, and Mark is granted a third visa that will last until we head back to Uganda in November of 2006 to finalize the adoption. The three-year foster period is quickly drawing to a close.

CHAPTER ELEVEN

April—May 2006, Canada

E IGHT MONTHS until we leave. Now is the time for me to throw myself deep into the confusing and challenging waters of international adoption bureaucracy.

I have read through a number of adoption handbooks and encountered an endless stream of testimonies on the internet regarding international adoption, but I find absolutely nothing about how to facilitate an adoption between Uganda and Canada. I phone a local adoption agency, hoping they can give me some advice.

243

"I have never heard of a situation like yours," the agency representative tells me. "You'd better just go back to Uganda and do it from there."

This is not what I want to hear. I long to talk to someone who has been through a similar adoption. I am desperate for help with how to walk through each step of the process, desperate to know what the steps even are.

My biggest impediment is the fact that Uganda has not ratified the Hague Adoption Convention, which created a set of standard procedures regarding international adoption. These standards exist for two main reasons: to protect children from trafficking and abduction by attempting to ensure only children who are legitimately eligible for adoption are adopted, and to help countries regulate the process of international adoptions. Because Uganda is not part of the Hague Conference, my only option is to follow the route of private international adoption.

In a private adoption between two countries that do not share mutual requirements and policies, the prospective parents — or parent — have the challenging task of fulfilling two different sets of legal requirements. Each country will only issue legal consent if and when they have received a certain degree of assurance from the other that they are also supportive of the adoption. Therefore, the Canadian government will not approve the adoption until after the Ugandan government approves it, and the Ugandan High Court will not approve it unless I have documentation testifying that Canada is supportive of the adoption. This process can become an endless cycle, trying to make both countries happy.

As I research more about international adoption, I learn that adoption has grown in conjunction with wars, refugee migrations, famines, and other natural disasters. I also come across some strong opinions against adoption. One source argues that adoption encourages children to be viewed as commodities and promotes corrupt practices, while another argues that adoption does not address the underlying issue of poverty. A third common argument I see is that international adoption further entrenches the dichotomy of power between rich and poor countries and diverts energy and resources that could be used more effectively toward alleviating this dichotomy.

Yet none of these arguments offers a convincing solution for the millions of orphans who are dying of malnutrition, disease, and poverty. Surely we must do all we can to protect children from becoming orphans in the first place, while simultaneously seeking to support and love the many children who are without families.

When confronted with disheartening statistics on the number of orphans both in one's own country and abroad, I find it easy to feel overwhelmed and to wonder how the actions or contributions of one person could possibly make a difference. But I must remember that these statistics don't encompass millions of faceless little children; rather, they refer to individuals, beautiful individuals who are fearfully and wonderfully made and who need, more than food or shelter or clothing or education, a family and a place to call home.

The term "international adoption" applies not to a crowd of faceless orphans, but rather to one baby: one boy or one girl. International adoption is a way through which one family opens their arms to love, cherish, and support one child.

It is timely when, one day after I have the disheartening conversation with the adoption agency, I receive a letter from Mr. Makiywe. In the letter, he responds to questions I asked him about the things I need to do in Canada in preparation for our return to Uganda in November. He writes:

Dear Ms. Tandela,

I wish to acknowledge the receipt of your two letters on the update of Mark and some clarifications on his adoption procedures in the Uganda Courts of Law.

On point, my office is responsible in the processing of the Adoption Orders in the Courts of Law (High Court) with the assistance of an Advocate (Lawyer) whom I have to contact on your behalf.

You will be required to pay a fee to the Lawyer for the processing of the Adoption Orders and could cost you $2000.

You are requested to have a Home Study about yourself and some recommendation letters from some referees/organizations. The possibility of booking the court date can be fixed in September 2006 so long as you confirm your coming.

Otherwise I do personally appreciate the good work as far as Mark's pictures portray.

I wish to hear from you soon and wish you good times with Mark.

God bless you!!
Nelson Makiywe
Probation Officer/Jinja

Mr. Makiywe's letter helps a bit. It confirms that I need a home assessment, which the Canadian government requires as well, letters of support, and a lawyer, who will arrange a court date in Uganda for roughly two thousand dollars. Other than that, I still have no idea what to do. I have a feeling there are many other requirements the Ugandan government may need in order to grant the adoption of Mark. I trust that Mr. Makiywe would not deliberately lead me astray, but I have learned through experience that he is not very detail-oriented, and thus I must not assume that the process is as straightforward as he makes it out to be.

We only have one shot at this, Mark and I. We cannot arrive in Uganda and learn that we are short a crucial document, because we have no way of getting back to Canada together, no guarantee that once we leave Canada we will both be able to return. I have to do this right the first time.

I find a government website that lists the requirements a prospective parent must fulfill:

Residency Requirements: Unless a judge waives the fostering requirements, prospective adoptive parents must reside in Uganda with their prospective adoptive child for three years. This means that a foreign citizen may adopt a Ugandan child if the foreigner has resided in Uganda for at least three years, and has also fostered the child for 36 months.

Age Requirements: Applicants must be at least 25 years old and 21 years older than the child they plan to adopt. In the case of a married couple, it is sufficient for one spouse to meet these requirements.

Marriage Requirements: Married couples must adopt jointly. Single parents may adopt, but they may not adopt a child of the opposite sex (unless an exception is made).

Income Requirements: There are no specific income requirements for Ugandan adoption, although prospective adoptive parents must be able to prove financial stability.

Other: Foreign adoptive parents must demonstrate they have no criminal record, and that they have been approved by their country of nationality to adopt.*

---

* *From http://adoption.state.gov/country_information/country_specific_info. php?country-select=uganda, accessed 2013.*

As of today, I can only claim that I have fulfilled three of the five Ugandan requirements. The first is the age requirement. I am more than twenty-one years older than Mark (I am twenty-two years and two months older), and I will be twenty-five years old when I apply to adopt Mark. The other requirement I have fulfilled is becoming financially stable and able to provide for Mark. With the job I have now, along with Mom and Dad's commitment to support us as needed, this shouldn't be a problem. I don't have a criminal record, and hopefully I will be approved by Canada to adopt in time.

That leaves two final stipulations. And I cannot fulfill either of them. Instead of fostering Mark in Uganda for thirty-six months, I have fostered him in Canada for most of this time. Second, I am not married, and Mark and I are obviously not the same sex. The judge can either hold these things against me, refusing me adoption rights, or make an exception to the rule.

I stare at Uganda's prerequisites for adoption, confronted with the reality that, according to Ugandan law, my case for adoption is very weak. The truth is that to award me legal adoption rights, a judge is going to have to grant me exemption from not one but two of the legal requirements.

It would be logical for me to be filled with a sense of hopelessness at this news, and yet I am filled with a peace that can only be explained as from God. It is a peace borne out of the truth that God is sovereign and knew beforehand that I would face these difficulties. Psalm 9 begins with the verse, "I will give thanks to the LORD with my whole heart; I will recount all of your wonderful deeds." When I reflect on all the miracles God brought about to bring Mark and me to Canada, I am strengthened with the hope that further miracles lie ahead.

Though on paper I am a far cry from an ideal candidate, I believe that God has the power to soften a judge's heart, and open his or her eyes to the unique truths that make up our story. The truth of how I met this precious boy who was discovered as a newborn in a pit latrine. The truth of how I cared for his tiny body when he was so sick and close to death. And the greatest truth of all: how over the last two and a half years our bond has grown to be no less strong than any mother and son of the same flesh. I pray these truths will be enough to convince the Ugandan authorities that I am a suitable candidate to adopt.

Using the internet as my only resource, I begin to piece together the specific legal logistics for Uganda.

First, I have to file a petition with the Ugandan High Court notifying them of my intentions to adopt. Second, I have to somehow locate a lawyer in Uganda who will act as my attorney and will book a court date for me in Kampala. Third, I have to ensure that the probation officer in charge of my case, Mr. Makiywe, submits a report to the court with his recommendation, or better yet, agrees to provide a testimony in person. I figure that three weeks is an acceptable time frame to accomplish these tasks, so in my mind I plan that we will go to Uganda for four weeks this November. I assume this will give us more than enough time to accomplish all we need to do.

I WAIT UNTIL May to schedule the home assessment because I want it to be conducted within six months of our departure. I pick up the phone and call Christian Adoption Services. A receptionist answers and asks how she may direct my call. I explain that I'd like to speak to someone about arranging a home assessment report, and she transfers me to a social worker.

I explain my situation to the social worker and then inquire, "How soon can I get a home assessment report completed?"

"Hmm... let's see here," she pauses on the other end

of the line. "All prospective parents are first required to take the parent preparation class, but from what you tell me you have been parenting Mark for over two years so we can probably get you exempted from that. In regard to the actual assessment," she continues, "there is quite a long waiting list right now. There is a form online that you have to fill out prior to booking an appointment, and once we review that we will call you to schedule a home assessment."

"If I get the form in tomorrow do you have any idea of when the assessment would be?"

"I'd estimate in around six months."

"Six months?" I repeat, aghast.

"Yes, give or take a month," she replies, oblivious to my dismay. "There are a lot of applications ahead of you and we've been averaging about six months from the request of the visit to the actual visit."

"Is there anything I can do in the meantime? I have to leave for Uganda in November, and I need the assessment to be completed and approved before I go."

I try to keep my voice steady as tears fill my eyes. While one hand grips the phone to my ear, the other folds into a tight fist, trying to confine the panic that threatens to invade every inch of my body. Six months puts us into October. That is cutting it way too close.

"I see," she says slowly. "Yes, that would be an almost impossible timeline because once the social worker has submitted their report it then takes an average of twenty working days for the report to be assessed and then approved or disapproved. So it all depends on when your report is actually submitted. In regard to your question, no, there is nothing you can do in the meantime other than to ensure that you have fulfilled the Ugandan requirements."

I hang up the phone in anguish and sink to my knees. *Please, Lord, work this out for us. Please, God, intervene.* God has patiently shown me time and time again that I need to completely place my trust in him rather than in the advice and cautionary words of well-meaning people. However, I constantly struggle with believing that God is going to work this out in our favour.

Will it ever be enough? I wonder. Will I ever get to the point where I stop doubting that God is going to come through? The point where I stop being plagued with the despairing thought that I will inevitably encounter a mountain that God will not be powerful enough to move? I recall the words of Jesus in response to a father's request that he heal his demon-possessed son:

Jesus asked the boy's father, "How long has he been like this?" "From childhood," he answered. "It has often thrown him into fire or water to kill him. But if you can do anything, take pity on us and help us." "'If you can'?" said Jesus. "Everything is possible for one who believes." Immediately the boy's father exclaimed, "I do believe; help me overcome my unbelief!"

(Mark 9:21-24)

Help me, Jesus. Help me overcome my unbelief!

CHAPTER TWELVE

May–November 2006, Canada

W E ALL get serious about the details now, knowing that we already have one tight deadline to work with: the home assessment. My dad somehow connects with a successful immigration lawyer named James Sheraton. In May, Dad, James, and I meet for lunch. I am hoping that over the course of this meeting James can give me some pointers on how to get started on the process. It would be amazing to have someone like him help me the whole way along, but there is no way that I can afford him. James arrives at our lunch dressed in an expensive dark blue suit. He is in his mid-forties, and his dark brown hair has begun to turn a distinguished grey above his ears.

"We want to go back to Africa to finish the adoption in November of this year," I tell him. "Do you have any tips on how I should go about this?"

"One error a lot of people make," James begins, "is they forget about preparing the immigration work beforehand. Instead, all the focus is on the adoption part. But if you wait until after the adoption is approved to work on the immigration papers, you have to go to the Canadian Embassy in Nairobi, file a request for Mark's residency, and then wait months and months to have it processed. So," he instructs me, "send in Mark's request for permanent residency well ahead of time. It will be incomplete until you have the official letter from Canada recognizing the adoption, but at least it will be in the pipeline." He pauses, leans back in his chair, and briefly glances at his watch. "Can you tell me your story from the beginning?"

I decide to give him an abbreviated version. I want to make sure I can get through more of my questions before our lunch is over.

When I finish, James takes a sip of water, sets it back down on the table, and runs his hand through his hair. His brow creases in deep contemplation. I watch as his eyes stare vacantly at the wall behind him and then pull into focus as he shifts his gaze directly at me. "Why don't I just help you?" he says, breaking the silence.

"I really appreciate the offer, but I can't afford it," I admit, a little sheepish. James's services would cost me thousands of dollars.

"No, I mean that I will help you at no cost. I really believe in what you are doing." I almost drop my water glass in disbelief. Before I can utter an answer, a smile broadens my face, and I close my eyes, uttering a short but very sincere prayer of thanksgiving for what my ears have just heard. *Thank you, Lord.*

My eyes open to both men meeting my gaze and awaiting my answer. "Thank you, James, that'd be wonderful."

James's office sends me a large envelope full of forms along with an extensive list of instructions on how to fill them out. His office will look after sending the completed forms to the Case Processing Centre in Mississauga, Ontario. Once this office approves me as Mark's "sponsor," they will forward the application to Nairobi. When I finally finish compiling all the supporting documents for Mark's permanent residency application, the pile of papers is impressive. And this is not just any pile of papers: This pile contains the history of both of our lives.

The application is now complete except for the adoption order letter from Canada declaring that the Canadian government legally recognizes the adoption. Canada will not issue this letter until they receive a letter of confirmation from the Ugandan High Court stating that Uganda has first recognized the adoption. Because of this, I include in the residency application a letter that explains that I will fax in the adoption order from Canada to the High Commission in Kenya as soon as we receive it so that it can be added to Mark's dossier prior to our arrival in Nairobi to pick up Mark's permanent residence card.

I am hoping that, like James said, this will eliminate the possibility that we are forced to wait in Nairobi for months for Mark's residency paperwork to be approved. Yet I cannot shake the discomfort brought on by one of the first sentences in a letter James's office enclosed with the application forms. It says: "The biggest obstacle is the visa office in Nairobi, which is not known for being facilitative."

It makes me nervous that the authorities who have the final say on whether or not Mark can return home with me have a world-wide reputation for being un-helpful. I have absolutely no interest in finding out firsthand what this really means.

ONCE AGAIN, GOD provides. In September I find a lawyer in Uganda who is willing to take on my case. I was put in touch with this lawyer through Peter, my friend who helped me get Mark's passport with his connection at the Kampala passport office. Since everything weighs on our appearance at the Ugandan High Court, I am encouraged to have secured a reliable, local attorney named Moses Ugama.

"I will look after booking a court date for you," he informs me. "It will cost four thousand five hundred dollars. But I will ensure that you have all your Ugandan paperwork ready for the hearing. However, you must know that I cannot provide any help with the Canadian paperwork you are to complete before you come here."

This is an important point. The Ugandan judge may find everything in order and be willing to grant me adoption rights, but if he or she doesn't have a document from the Canadian government affirming that they are also in support of this adoption, it will all be in vain.

AFTER AN AGONIZING wait, the adoption agency finally calls me to schedule a home assessment. The first interview is arranged for October 11th. It will take place at Mom and Dad's, where we are still living. The social worker has requested that both Mom and Dad be present as well as Mark.

I open the door to a young woman in her early thirties. Her blond hair is tied in a neat ponytail. She wears a blue cotton sweater and brown cords. Her name is Amanda, and she exudes a warmth that puts me at ease. I guide her up the stairs to the living room where Mom and Dad are waiting on the couch while Mark, now three and a half years old, plays on the floor with a couple of his trucks. He is singing softly.

"I can always tell where Mark is," I turn to her with a grin, "because he is always singing or talking to himself."

Mark has grown into a strong and tall little boy. His long, agile limbs have continued to show athletic promise, and his current favourite sport is hockey. He started preschool one month ago in September, just two mornings a week, and loves it. He has developed into quite the social butterfly, and at home he is constantly talking about his friends at school. He continues to see Kirsten's son, Koen, fairly often and remains like a big brother to him. Like most three-year-olds, he is very inquisitive and his eyes are often wide with excitement when he figures out a new skill or gains further understanding about how something works. He communicates very well, though when he talks really fast sometimes only I can recognize what he is trying to say. Along with sports, he adores anything related to music, something we both share.

I offer Amanda a seat and introduce her to Mom and Dad. After exchanging the usual pleasantries, she begins the interview.

"I read the four reference letters that you provided," she informs us. "They've been very helpful in shedding light on your situation. My first question is, how would you describe yourself, Tandela?"

Though the question seems harmless in itself, I am reminded of the weighty influence this interview will have on whether or not Canada grants me legal adoption rights. As soon as the words are out of her mouth, I feel my anxiety heighten. The late hours I have spent making sure I have all the paperwork in place for our trip next month, all the t's crossed and i's dotted, are taking their toll on me. The stress of the upcoming trip is amplified because the home assessment took forever to be scheduled. I try not to think about the fact that there is no guarantee that the assessment is going to be reviewed and approved before our flight to Uganda. Or that it might not be favourable. I have no idea what we will do if that happens. Our three-year foster probation period will be up in December, and therefore we must go to Uganda next month. But we cannot proceed with the adoption in Uganda without this report.

I feel like responding to Amanda's question with, "Since you asked, at this moment I would describe myself as nervous, tired, and scared of the unknown — did I say nervous and tired?" But I know what she means. She wants to know how I would describe myself in general, not in regard to the present stressful circumstances.

"I would say I am outgoing, friendly, and caring," I answer while simultaneously bouncing Mark up and down on my knee.

"And would you describe yourself as an introvert or extrovert?" Amanda asks.

"I'm an extrovert," I quickly respond. That's an easy one. "I love to be with people."

"And what would you say is a weakness of yours?" This is beginning to feel like a job interview, and one that is very awkward considering I am with my parents in their living room.

"I think I struggle with trying to be all things to all people. I'm learning how to say no. Being a parent is helping with that because I'm forced to say no to things that would take away from my time with Mark." Amanda glances down and makes a couple of notes in her journal. She leans toward me with encouraging eyes.

"How would you say you deal with pressure? Do you become stressed fairly easily?"

"I think people who know me would agree that I am pretty easygoing and laid-back. I don't get stressed out too easily. The last time that I was really stressed out was when I was working on getting the documents for Mark to travel back to Canada with me."

"And that is entirely understandable," Amanda reassures me. "I think that experience attests to your ability to handle large amounts of pressure. Most people would have crumbled under the circumstances. What are some ways you deal with stress on a daily basis?"

I share of my love for music and singing. It has been three years since I was last part of a worship team at church, and hopefully one day I can be a part of something like that again.

"I also love basketball," I add. Since I was ten years old I have been playing on some sort of basketball team.

I played all throughout high school and then for McGill University's varsity team. Even in Jinja I played a couple of times with boys who attended the same school as Sharon. There is a women's league that plays in the evenings near my parents' house. I would like to join, perhaps in one or two years when Mark is old enough that he would enjoy sitting through my games.

The interview concludes with Amanda conducting a detailed walk-through of the home. She writes down particulars regarding each room in the house, where people sleep, and what the yard is like. I am struck by the irony that many children in this city grow up in living arrangements that leave much to be desired while those who provide a safe home have their arrangements scrutinized by professionals.

The second interview is conducted two days later at the agency's office. This time only Mark and I are present. During this interview, Amanda questions me further about my personal life.

"Are you currently in a dating relationship?"

"No."

"And have you ever lived common-law with anyone?"

"No."

"When were you last in a relationship, if ever?"

"That would be three years ago, before I left for Uganda." My life before motherhood seems a lifetime ago.

"Who then would you say is a male role model for Mark?" She continues to dig into this sensitive topic, reminding me over and over that I am a single mom.

"I make it a priority for Mark to spend time with his grandpa, Uncle Nathan, and Uncle Kelly. I hope one day to marry and provide Mark with a father." I hope; oh, how I hope.

Amanda stares at me momentarily. In her eyes I think I detect a hint of sadness. Or is it pity?

"I see. And your parents, how would you describe their marriage?"

"Their marriage is honest, open, loving, and balanced. I think they complement one another well, something I feel is important in every marriage. They have their Christian faith in common and a strong belief that marriage is for life."

My mom and dad are hard workers, both in and outside the home. Talking about their marriage with Amanda amplifies my grief at having nothing to say about my own. I wish I could boast about my husband, about how good he is with Mark and how much Mark loves him. Amanda has had to make some adjustments to the questions she is asking me because most of them are designed for a couple. Will Mark ever call someone Daddy? I look at my little boy, deep in concentration as he plays with Lego in a corner of the room, and experience a pang of sorrow. I know the ideal arrangement for a child is to have a mother and a father, and I am deeply sad that all I can offer Mark is me.

"Tandela? I asked you to describe your mom and dad for me."

I try to focus. I take a deep breath. How am I to describe my parents in a few sentences, especially when I know each word is weighed so heavily? I begin with Mom, and how she is selfless, loving, and giving, always placing her family's needs first, perhaps too much so at times. I share how she spends a great deal of time with her two grandsons and is a huge help to Kirsten and me in that respect.

My dad is patient, calm, and sensitive. He has a really big heart and deeply cares for those in need. He models what it means to live out your convictions.

"In regard to parenting, is there anything you will do differently from your parents?"

I take time to gather my thoughts. I know what the answer is, but I want to choose my words carefully. It became evident soon after Mark and I moved in that

I was more intent on enforcing boundaries and carrying out discipline than Mom and Dad were. Which makes complete sense. They are Mark's grandparents, not his parents. Grandparents are not supposed to be the disciplinarians. They do not have to be strict like they were with their own children, because they do not deal directly with the repercussions of "spoiling." But most children only visit their grandparents—they don't usually live with them.

Since Mark and I live in the same house as Mom and Dad, it has been a challenge to teach Mark that certain things are not acceptable even though my mom and dad allow them. And Mom and Dad were definitely not strict parents to Kirsten, Nathan, and me. In retrospect, I think that they may have been too relaxed with us, that we could have used more boundaries and discipline in our youth. Amanda nods, then scribbles down some notes.

Glancing back up, the tip of her pen still on her notepad, she asks, "How do you try to teach Mark about boundaries, about right and wrong?"

"As a parent I believe that my job is to nurture, guide, and teach Mark. I think that children are gifts from God, and I want to help direct Mark to make the best choices possible while guiding him to become who God wants him to be. I feel blessed to be Mark's mother and have him in my life. I guess you could say I'm 'traditional' in the sense that I don't think a child should run the home. Of course I aim to lavish Mark with love and affection, but this doesn't mean he will always get his own way. Sometimes the most loving thing I can do for him is to say no.

"I hope Mark will learn to value other people for who they are and naturally develop a desire to help those who are less fortunate. I hope to teach Mark about the God who loves him and created him, and help Mark grow and develop his own genuine faith."

I am at ease talking about my faith because I know that Amanda is from a Christian agency. Regardless of whether she is or not, I would say the same thing, but knowing we share a common belief in Jesus makes me feel less vulnerable.

"When discipline is needed, I place Mark in his bedroom for a time-out. Or he may get a time-out from a particular privilege, such as a toy. The two of us talk about why the behaviour was inappropriate and how Mark can handle things better in the future. I think it is just as important to reinforce positive behaviour, so I make a point of encouraging him when he is doing well."

She looks at me intently and, changing the subject, asks me to describe how Mark is with other people.

"With people he knows, he is really friendly. He's more shy and cautious with people he's not familiar with." I explain. "I'd describe him as perceptive for a three-and-a-half-year-old, easygoing, and gentle."

"And what do you and Mark like to do together?"

"What do we like to do, buddy? What is that you are playing with?"

"A fire truck," he replies matter-of-factly, for he has now moved on from playing with Lego to his prized fire truck toy. "And this is my book," he says, picking up a favourite book of his I brought along.

"Do you like to play the drums, Mark?" I ask him.

"Yes!"

"One of his favourite activities is to play on his makeshift drum set. It consists of a toy drum, a yoga ball, and a cutting board," I explain to Amanda.

"And do you like to play sports, Mark?" I ask, turning back to him.

He nods vigorously.

"What sports do you like to play?"

"I like to play, umm..." he pauses. "I like to play hockey. I can skate!" He proudly declares to Amanda. Last winter when it got cold enough to use the outdoor rink across the street, Nathan began teaching Mark how to skate.

"Yes, that's right. And how about basketball? Do you like to play basketball?"

"Yes. I like basketball, too. And my horse!"

I ruefully chuckle at this statement. Amanda looks at me with a quizzical but amused look.

"Yes, you love your *rocking* horse," I clarify, sharing a smile with Amanda. "We also like to play at the park; there's one right across the street. And Mark also really enjoys swimming. Right now he is really interested in nature, and just yesterday he sat for an hour with Bumpy—that's what he calls my dad—while they looked up photos of all kinds of different animals online. And we are learning new words and practicing how to count." I kneel down next to Mark on the floor. "How old are you, Mark? Can you show me with your fingers?" Mark proudly holds up all of his fingers. I chuckle. "That's not three! That's ten, you silly goose."

"I am ten!" he exclaims excitedly.

"No, you aren't ten. Are you three?" I tickle his tummy and flash him a knowing smile.

"Yes," he admits, a little dejectedly.

"Show me how many fingers."

Mark thrusts three fingers in the air, showing he understands, his smile suddenly returning.

"Oh buddy, you are too much." I affectionately stroke his hair. It is growing into quite the 'fro and could use a haircut. I put the fire truck back in front of him and return to my chair by Amanda.

"Now, in your own words, tell me why you want to adopt Mark. From the beginning. Wait — is it okay to do this in front of him?" Amanda says, nodding in Mark's direction.

"Yes," I respond. "I've no intention of keeping Mark's story a secret from him. I have spoken with Mark about what it means to be adopted and how we are going back to Uganda to finish this process."

From the beginning, Amanda said. I look at my watch. We have approximately twenty more minutes left in the interview. I give her a brief but accurate account of how I met Mark, came to care for him, and then felt called to adopt him. Amanda smiles as I finish the story. Much has happened in such a short amount of time. It becomes increasingly evident to me just how amazing our story is each time I share it.

"And how did you like your time in Uganda?"

"I loved it. I made some good friends there. I'm really glad I got to spend a decent amount of time there, in

Mark's birth country, because I think it is really important that I teach Mark about where he was born. I am proud of his culture and heritage, and I hope he will be, too. We've been going to a church where pretty much everyone is of African descent. If it weren't for that, Mark would hardly ever see another black person. He knows he looks different from everyone in our family." I begin to chuckle. "He says we are vanilla and he's chocolate. But in all seriousness, I think it's healthy for him to have the opportunity to meet people who also have an African heritage and are proud of it."

After chatting with Mark a bit more about the toys he brought with him and the Lego tower he built during the past hour, Amanda concludes our interview. She assures me that she will have the home assessment report completed within one month. I pray this will be the case as we leave for Uganda in one month and five days.

THREE WEEKS AFTER the first interview, Amanda gives me her report for my review. I stare at the final sentence: "On the basis of this home assessment report, I recommend that Tandela Swann be approved to adopt Mark Kirab Swann, born in Uganda, who is currently living with Tandela in Canada."

This means that we almost have everything in place to be approved by the Ugandan authorities. I can hardly believe it. The last page of the report requires four signatures: Amanda's, her supervisor's, mine, and the Alberta Adoption Services manager's. After I add my signature, only one empty line remains. All that I need now is for Andrea Sutherland, the manager of Alberta Adoption Services, to read this report, give her approval, and issue me a letter of recommendation. This letter will serve as evidence to the Ugandan High Court that Canada is in favour of the adoption. Our plane leaves in fifteen days.

It is November 17th, 2006. There is one day left until our departure, and I still do not have the letter I need from Andrea. For the past two weeks I've woken up every day thinking, *Maybe today it will come. Please, Lord, send it today.* I have left a couple of messages with Andrea's office, based three hundred kilometres away in Edmonton, but haven't heard back. I can wait no longer, so I do a bit of detective work on the internet and come up with a number that may be her direct line.

"Good morning, this is Andrea," the voice on the other end of the line announces.

"Hi, Andrea. My name is Tandela Swann." I take a deep breath. I can't believe I've actually gotten through. "The reason I am calling is that I am leaving for Uganda tomorrow with my son and you have some paperwork in your office that needs to be signed before I go."

"How did you get this number?" She sounds shocked.

"I found it online," I reply. Before she can dismiss my call, I hurry through a brief synopsis of my desperate situation.

"I understand what you are saying," she speaks slowly. I can almost hear her trying to collect her thoughts. "But I can't just sign off on the report without reading it. There are certain procedures in place for this. I think you jumped about six steps by calling me directly. You have a lot of guts," she admits, audibly impressed by my determination. Then I hear her sigh. "What I am trying to tell you is that I will not be able to get you the signed report and a letter of recommendation, *should you receive one*," she emphasizes, "before you leave tomorrow. But I can promise you that I will begin reviewing your case today and will have my office send the results by priority mail to your home."

Don't have a breakdown, don't have a breakdown, I tell myself as I hang up the phone. Mark is sitting at the kitchen table eating a bowl of Cheerios. He is conscious that as the date of our departure draws nearer, I become more stressed. In turn, this causes him to act out more than usual. The last thing I want now is for him to watch his mother crumble into a heap of tears.

"What's wrong, Mommy?" he asks, his dark brown eyes full of concern.

"I am just making some arrangements for our trip tomorrow. Remember how I told you we are going on an airplane back to the place where you were born? To Uganda?"

Mark's hand pauses in midair as he brings a spoonful of Cheerios to his mouth. "Bumpy too?" he asks, referring to my dad.

"Yes, Bumpy is coming with us. That's right."

Because my parents don't want me going on this trip alone, Dad is taking a month off work to come with us.

"You need a male figure with you," Mom agreed. "And your dad, with him being a politician as well as a physician, it may be helpful."

I am glad Dad will be with us. I can't imagine dealing with the Ugandan bureaucracy on my own while simultaneously trying to look after Mark. I am already worried about how Mark will adapt to Uganda. He has no memories of it. In particular, I am wondering what will happen with his skin. Ever since he was a baby he has had issues with his skin, and these issues are exacerbated in the heat. Every morning I coat his little body in Vaseline to keep his skin from drying out and being itchy.

I look at Mark. He is focused on scooping up the last few Cheerios in his cereal bowl. I make a note to pack a large bag of Cheerios for our trip.

Mom enters the kitchen. "What did she say?"

"She says she'll start looking at it today but that I won't have it for when we leave tomorrow," I reply despondently. "She'll mail it here priority post when it is done," I explain, struggling to hold back my tears.

Mom stares hard at me. I recognize the look in her eyes. It is the same look I give Mark when I watch him play with other children and can't help but wonder how he will fit in when he is older. It is a look that comes out of my longing to protect him, to keep him innocent of the atrocities of the world, and the simultaneous realization that so much is out of my control.

"I can mail it for you."

"Mail it?" Are we talking about the same thing here? Snail mail all the way to Uganda? Maybe we should try a hot air balloon instead. *It would probably get there faster,* I think ruefully.

"Yes. I can FedEx it or something." She pauses, her eyes widening at the idea. "Does FedEx go to Uganda?"

My mother is brilliant.

I hurry downstairs to the computer. I scroll down the list of countries that FedEx delivers to. Turks and Caicos Islands, Tuvalu, U.S. Virgin Islands... Uganda. Yes. FedEx delivers to one location in Uganda, the Entebbe Airport. I call to see what the transit time will be.

The representative at the other end of the line tells me this is the first time he has looked into such a request. After briefly putting me on hold, he informs me that the delivery time will be approximately five business days, and it will cost $150.

I go over our itinerary in my mind. Immediately after we land at the Entebbe Airport, we head straight to Jinja to meet with the probation officer. There is no plan to return to Entebbe until we fly to Kenya to get Mark's permanent residency card—if the adoption goes through. I need to somehow get the letter from the airport to Jinja.

Once again, I call Sharon and ask for her help. Because she is presently studying in Kampala, she says it will be easy for her to pick up the letter in Entebbe when it arrives. Then she will get on the first bus to Jinja available.

"You are right, Mom," I announce triumphantly as I bound up the last stairs to the main floor. "FedEx will fly it to the airport where Sharon is going to pick it up and bring it to me, since I'll already be in Jinja meeting with the probation officer. We just have to pray that the letter gets there. It has to go from the Ministry's office in Edmonton to our house in Calgary, our house to the post office, post office to FedEx, then it has to travel thirteen thousand kilometres by air on a number of planes, and finally has to arrive in Entebbe, where Sharon has to pick it up and bring it to Jinja by bus."

As I say this, it registers how there are so many instances where the letter can go missing. It is such a small package. Without it, we have no case in court, for it is to serve as our official evidence to the Ugandan judge that the Canadian government is supportive of the adoption.

"If it gets lost, we are hooped." I feel my eyes widen and a knot form in my throat. "Then Dad goes home by himself, I guess. Mark won't be allowed to leave. But I will stay there for as long as is necessary to have the adoption granted."

"Of course, Tandy." Mom puts her arm around my shoulder and leans her head against my own. "He is your son. And from the day he arrived home in this house, he has been my grandson. Tandy, if it looks like you have to stay there, I will come over. I'll take time off work and come there and look after Mark while you get a job.

"It is better for Dad to go with you now; this is his thing. He is good in high-pressure situations. You know me, I can take care of all the details behind the scenes. How many times have I had to do something similar for your dad or Nathan? Something last-minute for them on which it felt like their whole life depended? My anxiety level will be off the charts, but we'll get it done somehow. No matter what happens, we are all in this together." She pulls out a chair and gestures for me to sit down.

"I know how it can be over there, Tandy, I have lived in developing countries, too. I know you feel strongly about refusing to cut any corners, about having to have a receipt for everything, but this time you may have to do something to get this done. You'll be in a different culture where there are certain expectations for that sort of thing. I just don't want you to get stuck," Mom shares, looking me squarely in the eyes.

"I can't, Mom. It goes against everything I have stood for up to this point. I know the system, but I can't support it. I have to find another way. I will not play that game."

I hope that I will never again be faced with such a decision — pay a bribe or lose Mark. How dare anyone pad their pocket by putting a price on my child? He is my son. I am his mother. No matter what anyone else decides, no matter what any official document says, that is who we are to each other. Mother and son.

"TANDY, IT'S NOT in the judge's hands alone," Kirsten reminds me gently. It is the night before we leave, and Kirsten, Kelly, and Koen have come to say goodbye. "I have no doubt that this is going to happen. It is going to go through," Kirsten shares confidently.

"We'll see." I shrug off her statements. Kirsten is the naïve one; I am the practical one. "There are a lot of obstacles I have to get through."

"It's hard to say goodbye again." Sitting cross-legged beside me in the living room, her big blue eyes fill with tears. "I wish I could go with you."

"Me too. But it's okay, Dad will be there."

"I just want to be a part of it, you know?"

"I'll send you emails, every chance I get," I promise her, resting my hand on her knee reassuringly.

"I'll be praying constantly, Tandy." Kirsten pauses, shifting slightly so she can look at me directly, her watery eyes now a shimmering sea of turquoise. "I just feel I need to tell you that none of this is outside of God's control. Don't forget about all that Jesus did in Uganda for you and Mark. You and Mark didn't get to come to Canada together because you were lucky. Mark was not pulled out of the pit latrine because he was lucky, because someone just happened to find him a few hours before death. There is a plan. Jesus' plan for Mark is bigger than you and bigger than any judge or court system. His plans for all of us are bigger and better than we could imagine."

These words I cannot shrug off.

CHAPTER THIRTEEN

November 2006, Uganda

W E ARRIVED at the Entebbe Airport outside of Kampala yesterday. I hadn't been on a plane since we left Uganda over two and a half years ago, and had forgotten how fatiguing international travel can be. I think the seats have shrunk considerably. Any energy reserves I had were used up trying to entertain Mark and keep him from going stir-crazy on the plane. Even though he is a fairly calm and relaxed child, he is still a three-year-old. Dad and I took turns hauling snacks out of our bags and playing with the small toys and books that I managed to fit in my carry-on.

An extremely stressful moment occurred when we were almost forced back to Canada. When we arrived in the U.K., the customs officer told me that Mark wasn't going to be able to get on our flight from London to Kampala because he didn't have a direct airside transit visa. Eventually he relented, and we were let through. All our luggage made it to Entebbe except for Mark's stroller.

If something as large as a stroller can go missing, what are the chances that our FedExed letter is going to make it here? Every day I check the status of the letter online. I purchased a cell phone the day after we arrived and will call Sharon as soon as the letter gets in.

After sleeping in a guest house near the airport last night, we took a mid-morning bus from Entebbe to Jinja. We are now standing in a line outside the Department of Probation and Social Welfare office. Mr. Makiywe's office is one of four located in a long and narrow single-storey building. Thankfully, a covered walkway extends off the front of the building, shielding us from the hot sun.

"I don't think we are going to get in," I dejectedly tell Dad. The three of us have been waiting for two hours to have a word with Mr. Makiywe and ensure he has prepared a letter of support to present to the

High Court in Mbale. Our lawyer, Mr. Ugama, has advised Mr. Makiywe to accompany us to the court appointment in Mbale to provide a verbal testimony of support. However, I am nervous that Mr. Makiywe may find an excuse not to join us in court, and if he doesn't come in person, the court requires he provide a letter that demonstrates his full support.

Mark has nestled himself into a corner toward the end of the building, his knees tucked up against his chest, and is spending the time snacking on Cheerios and flipping through a sticker book, pausing every so often to gaze at his new surroundings. He has been a bit quieter than usual since we arrived and is much more reserved in public. Mistaken for a local, Ugandans have addressed him in Luganda or Swahili a number of times already, and Mark stares blankly at them, unsure of how to respond.

Unfortunately, we are still in line when Mr. Makiywe's office closes. I walk dejectedly back to our hotel while Mark skips along, keeping up to Dad's long gait, the two of them soaking up the beauty of Jinja. My anguish over the delay in seeing Mr. Makiywe is exacerbated by the fact that I am still waiting for our lawyer, who is based in Mbale, to notify us of our court date. I had hoped he would have a court date in place for us before we left Canada (something he committed to in his initial letter to me), but he has not been able to book one yet. I am anxious to get to Mbale to meet him face-to-face. But first I have to get this letter from Mr. Makiywe.

Later that evening, the cheap cell phone I bought begins to ring. It's my mom, and she gives me the good news that the letter from Andrea has arrived at their house.

"Do you want me to open it?" she asks. I look over at Mark, who has moved from my side to sit on his bed with my dad for a bedtime story. I rise quickly and step into the hallway, closing the door behind me. My heart beats rapidly, for I am all too aware that if Andrea has decided she cannot support my request for adoption, it is all over and our trip will have been in vain. I summon the courage to tell Mom to read me what it says. She tears the envelope open and I hear the rustling of paper as she unfolds the letter.

"Enclosed please find an original 'To Whom It May Concern' letter, for presentation to the authorities in Uganda, indicating that you have met the criteria for adoption in Alberta." Mom pauses, allowing her words to sink in. A surge of relief rushes upon me, and I am unable to speak.

She continues on. "Please note that this adoption *must* be finalized in the child's country of origin and that Alberta Children's Services will have no role in facilitating this adoption."

Mom tells me that she will take it to the FedEx office today, for it is only mid-morning there. This means it will hopefully arrive in Uganda in five or six days. I guess in retrospect it is a good thing that our court date wasn't within the first week we arrived in Uganda, for without this letter, we would have had to cancel it. And there is no guarantee we would have been able to get another one within the next few weeks.

I recall what Jesus' brother James says when he warns people that they must remember the truth that God is not ruled by our plans, and cautions we not view our lives as though we are the orchestrators of all that we do, of where we go, or of time itself.

Now listen, you who say, "Today or tomorrow we will go to this or that city, spend a year there, carry on business and make money." Why, you do not even know what will happen tomorrow. What is your life? You are a mist that appears for a little while and then vanishes. Instead, you ought to say,

"If it is the Lord's will, we will live and do this or that."

(James 4:13-15)

These verses reinforce the truth that the adoption will not go through based on how organized I am or how closely we stick to my imaginary agenda. I know that it is okay to plan; however, I must hold my plans with an open hand, consistently surrendering them to God. I lie in bed, grateful that God has graciously allowed me to dwell on this truth, which actually brings me a great sense of freedom because it prompts me to lay the burden of the next three weeks down at God's feet.

"Thank you for that letter," I whisper softly, so as not to disturb Mark. "Help me to believe that your ways are good, especially in these circumstances where nothing seems to be going right," I pray. For the first time since we arrived here, I sleep soundly through the night.

The next morning, I am immediately given the opportunity to live out what God taught me the night before. We have returned to Mr. Makiywe's office, only to be informed by his secretary that he will not be in. I fight the urge to be filled with disappointment, and pray that God will direct us instead toward an activity that the three of us will enjoy. After all, out of the three of us, I'm the only one who really wanted to spend the morning in a cramped probation office.

I suggest to Dad that we go visit one of Jinja's famous sites, the entrance to the Nile River. From here, water travels over sixty-six thousand kilometres to Egypt. Our hotel provides us with a driver, and while we drive, I call our lawyer, Mr. Ugama, to inform him that we expect to have the letter of recommendation from Canada within the next week, and will bus to Mbale as soon as it arrives.

The area, known as the "Source of the Nile," is beautiful, and we manage to spend most of our day here, at Jinja's main tourist destination, which boasts stand after stand of locally made crafts, a number of boating and white-water rafting activities, and a good-sized open-air restaurant reminiscent of a North American brew pub. In the end, I am thankful because the day gives Mark an opportunity to further experience and appreciate the beauty of Jinja. I hope that this trip will allow Mark to have many positive associations with his birth country, and I am trying to take lots of photographs so that years from now his memory may be triggered by them.

THE THIRD TIME we go to Mr. Makiywe's office we get in. After a round of greetings and introductions between him and my dad, I inform Mr. Makiywe of the purpose of our visit, explaining we require a letter stating that he is in support of the adoption arrangement.

"Mmm-hmm." Mr. Makiywe pointlessly shuffles a stack of papers on his desk. "Do you see a computer or typewriter on my desk?"

I do not, but I know his secretary has one on hers.

"So how do you expect me to write the letter? You must go and write it for me and bring it back. Then I will decide if I think it is in Mark's best interest that I sign it."

His words hit me like a punch in the gut. Not because they are malicious, but rather because I am suddenly conscious that I should have anticipated this response from Mr. Makiywe. I should have known it would fall on my shoulders to type up this letter. This has always been the case in the past; why would this time be any different? I can't believe that in the last three days of waiting for this meeting the thought never crossed my mind. *You need to change your mentality,* I tell myself. *We are not in Canada anymore.*

If we are going to be successful in Uganda, I have to assume the perspective I had when I lived here two and a half years ago. I must anticipate unorthodox procedures and delays. I must assume that every day will be a fight to keep moving things forward. I have heard enough stories of people who have come here in similar situations only to face months and months of delays. I know the biggest opportunity for delay with adoptions is waiting to get a court date booked. What tends to happen is that a date gets booked and then at the last minute is changed because of something more urgent and is never rescheduled. It would have been more convenient for us to get an appointment with a judge at the Jinja High Court, but because our lawyer is based in Mbale and has influence with the judges there, he told us Jinja would not be an option.

After Mr. Makiywe has ushered the three of us out of his office, I start off in the direction of the internet café that I have frequented before. Dad is carrying Mark around because of our lost stroller, and we walk to the café with Mark sitting high on top of Dad's shoulders. As I anticipated, Mark's skin is very irritated by the heat. He is coping surprisingly well, perhaps distracted by the novelty of his new environment. I am grateful for Mark's easygoing nature. I wish I could be more focused on trying to make the trip lots of fun, but there is too much business to take care of. Thankfully, Mark is delighting in the one-on-one time he is getting from his Bumpy, and doesn't seem to notice how preoccupied I am.

While Mark and Dad each order a juice, I sit down at one of the Source Café's computers and type up Mr. Makiywe's letter. I read it over twice for grammatical errors, pay the cashier, and go back to Mr. Makiywe's office, leaving Dad and Mark to enjoy the refreshing air-conditioning.

"Thank you, Tandela," Mr. Makiywe says. A pen is poised in his hand above the letter, ready to sign it. "That will be fifty dollars, please."

"Fifty dollars?" I echo. "For your signature?"

I am confused. He didn't have to do any work. I am the one who wrote the letter. Is this a bribe? I need that letter signed, but I cannot risk being involved in any illegitimate activity.

"I will be happy to stamp this with my approval for the small fee of fifty dollars." He pauses, handing the letter back to me. "It is a small cost to pay for my support."

I don't know what to do. I need time to think about this.

"I don't have that kind of money with me," I confess, hoping to buy some time.

"Well, you come back when you do, and I will be happy to help you." Mr. Makiywe's words are firm.

There is one person that may be able to help sort this out for me. Her name is Naomi, and she works as a probation officer in Mbale. I met her when I lived in Mbale during my first month in Uganda. Naomi has an outstanding reputation as an honest probation officer, and I know I can rely on her to give me sound advice on what I need to do in this particular situation. Naomi spends a great deal of time helping Ugandans understand the need for local adoption, and she strives to do everything in her power to keep the adoption process straightforward and accessible to locals. I hope her cell phone number has not changed in the last three years.

The phone rings six times, and I fear that I have the wrong number. Suddenly I hear her voice.

After inquiring about how her family is doing, and filling her in on why I am back in Uganda, I ask for her help regarding Mr. Makiywe.

"I don't want to be taken advantage of, and I don't want to rely on bribery to move things forward. I don't want to be cheated, but I also don't want to cheat him," I explain to her. "What do you recommend is the most appropriate thing to do? It's not about the money,"

I continue, "It's about knowing what things I should legally pay for."

"I understand, Tandela," Naomi replies. "You are not from here, and because of this, the authorities will expect you to pay for certain services that, while they are generally free for locals, are not free for foreigners."

Her comment reminds me of when Sharon, Mark, and I went to the wildlife reserve in Entebbe a couple of days before our flight home to Canada and the price of admission for non-Ugandans was four times the cost of admission for Ugandans.

"So there are two systems?" I ask, confused.

"I think a better way of putting it is that there are different standards," Naomi corrects me. "And I would say that paying a small fee to have your letter signed is legitimate."

After receiving this counsel from Naomi, whom I trust completely, I go back to Mr. Makiywe and pay him the money with a clear conscience.

NOW THAT WE have the letter from Mr. Makiywe, the only thing holding us back from going to Mbale is waiting for the FedExed letter to arrive. Our hotel room is small, with two single beds and a tiny bathroom. Dad has his own room next door to us. The cramped space is dimly lit, so we spend as much time as we can outside of our rooms. The hotel's dining area is quite large, and we are welcome to hang out there even between meals. Mark always looks forward to his breakfast, as it is a treat for him to start the day off with juice. Since today is our first day in Jinja without an agenda, I decide to take Mark and Dad to visit the orphanage.

At around ten o'clock we begin a leisurely walk from our hotel to the orphanage. The road is slightly damp from the heavy rain that fell while we were sleeping. The aromas of the air are intensified by the blanket of moisture that covers the grass and the porous, dark red soil. Leaves droop slightly, weighed down by precipitation. Our hair is dampened by the occasional raindrop that slowly trickles from the trees above.

As we walk, I explain once again to Mark that we are going to visit the place where he and I first met. "There are a lot of people here that are excited about seeing you," I tell him with an encouraging smile. "I know you won't remember this place, but the women who work here will remember you."

Mark is aware that the purpose of our trip here is to finalize the adoption. While I have spoken to him much about what it means to be adopted, I have protected him from the details of our trip, telling him only that we are here to finalize some paperwork. We have a scrapbook at home that is full of photos from his first year at the orphanage, and we go through it together all the time.

"Will I see the swing that I liked so much?" He looks at me with curious eyes. "Yes, if it is still there," I reply. When Mark was a baby he loved to be pushed in a blue bucket swing.

Before we reach the main gate, shouts and shrieks from children beginning their outdoor playtime greet our ears. I introduce myself to the young man who has replaced Solomon as the orphanage's guard. The hectic activity within the yard is a familiar sight to my eyes: children zooming around on tricycles while others holler at one another as they play tag, and a group of housemothers and children attempting to play a game of duck-duck-goose. I notice that the area hosts a new swing set and a small playground. In addition to tricycles, there are small plastic cars that the children can sit in and steer around, propelled by the movement of their feet below. I called Margaret this morning to inform her of our visit, and she has been waiting expectantly, walking toward us with open arms.

"It has been so long!" she exclaims, releasing me from her embrace to take in how Mark has grown. She stretches out her hand and introduces herself to him, explaining that though he doesn't remember her, she remembers much from the year he spent here as a baby. Mark nods, familiar with Margaret's name as I have spoken much of her over the past two years. He leans against my leg, silently taking in the chaotic scene before him with wide eyes.

I introduce Margaret to my dad, who by now has been surrounded by a number of children, all tugging at him and beckoning for him to come and play with them. Most of the Caucasian visitors here are female; Dad's presence is therefore an anomaly. I let the kids pull Dad away while I fill Margaret in on what we have been up to since we arrived and our approximate timeline for the rest of the trip. Recognizing it may take some time for Mark to get over his shyness, Margaret asks us if we would like a tour.

I squeeze Mark's hand. "That sounds like fun." I beckon for Dad to follow, and Margaret leads the three of us inside.

As we move from room to room, I notice that although there haven't been any structural changes, most of the walls have been repainted and many of the beds have been replaced. The furniture in the dining room is also new. I mention this to Margaret, and she informs me that within the last year they have received some financial assistance from a few churches in the United States that have allowed them to make some much-needed updates to the home. She grows quiet when we enter the babies' dorm, respectfully allowing me to take it in and explain to Dad and Mark the significance of this room.

I slip my hand out of Mark's grasp and walk over to where his crib used to be, for this room has also been equipped with new furniture. "This is where you slept," I say softly, my hands resting on the edge of the wooden frame. "You and Teddy," I add. "You shared this crib with another little boy until you were nine months old, when you came and lived with me."

Dad moves quietly through the room, his hands gliding over each passing bed. Just as before, every crib has another stacked on top of it, mimicking actual bunk beds. My memories of my first few days here are vivid. I remember how overwhelmed and inadequate I felt when I was given the responsibility of overseeing the ten sickest children. I can still picture rocking Mark in my arms and trying to get him to sleep. Those were the days when he stared blankly for hours into space without making eye contact with anyone.

Mark looks up, and I am aware that I have been lost

in my thoughts, a pensive expression taking over my face. Meeting his gaze, I quickly break into a smile, for I don't want Mark to perceive that being reminded of how he began his life makes me sad. Truthfully, instead of being filled with sorrow, this visit has brought me great joy because it is an acute reminder of how unfathomable Mark's story is. And it brings me hope for the rest of the children here, hope that God will continue to provide for and intervene in miraculous ways in their lives, just as he has in Mark's.

I ask Margaret if any of the children have been adopted since I left. She tells me that two of the babies here are in the process of being adopted by separate families in the U.S.

"Since you left there has been one instance where a local Ugandan family inquired about adoption," she shares. "But when they went to process the foster parent paperwork, they were informed by the probation office that it would cost a fee equivalent to five hundred U.S. dollars. They were incredibly disheartened, for they had been visiting this particular child for weeks and were extremely attached. But they did not have the money."

Margaret admits the situation was extremely frustrating, and reinforces the understanding that adoption is something only to be considered by the rich. This is one of the current reasons why the majority of orphans in Uganda are adopted by families overseas.

"It shouldn't be this way," she shakes her head, the scar on her right cheek more apparent as she frowns. "It should be easier for locals to adopt. The Bible says we are to care for the fatherless and motherless, yet how are families here supposed to do this when the authorities make it nearly impossible?" She pauses and closes her eyes briefly, composing herself in the midst of her obvious disappointment. She rolls her shoulders back and her eyes flash with a look of determination I have come to know well. "Let's move outside," she suggests, smiling a warm, toothy grin that spreads across her face when she looks at Mark. "I know there are some housemothers there who would love to see you."

We spend the rest of the hour outside with Margaret and watch as a couple of the housemothers assist the cook with preparing lunch on the outdoor stove. Margaret invites us to stay for lunch, after which Mark joins some of the three- and four-year-olds in the front yard. He spends most of his time on one of the swings, carefully observing the commotion around him. He moves with a quiet self-assurance, perceptive beyond his years. I wonder what he is thinking as he tries to absorb all the details of this place where he spent the first year of his life. It is hard to believe at times that such a tall and strong three-and-a-half-year-old started out very small and sickly, the tiniest of all the children here. Not only did he defy the odds of having a life-threatening disease, in the two and a half years that we have been away Mark has developed into a little boy who ranks at the top of the growth chart for his age. Though he is a year younger than some of the other children at the orphanage, he is physically the biggest.

The housemothers who tenderly cared for Mark during his first year of life were quite attached to him. They remember taking Mark in when he was released from the hospital, and they did everything they could, with the limited knowledge and resources they had at their disposal, to keep him alive. I will always be grateful for how they cared for him. Before we leave, Mark patiently endures hugs and kisses from a number of these housemothers. I say my goodbyes as well, for I do not know if I will ever return. I promise Margaret I will let her know how the adoption hearing goes.

She walks us to the gate. Taking my hand in hers, she says solemnly, "I will be praying for you. It is going to go well for you, Tandela, I am sure of this." She bends down to look Mark directly in the eyes. "Thank you for coming here today, Mark. We were all greatly looking forward to it. And I'm sure you know this," she adds, her hand resting on his head with great affection, "but you have a very special mother."

"I know," Mark acknowledges matter-of-factly, as though Margaret has just announced that the sky is blue. I chuckle quietly at his response, treasuring the innocent directness of a three-year-old.

Dad thanks Margaret for her hospitality and for her unwavering support of Mark and me over the years. We head out under a pure azure sky, our three pairs of footprints faintly visible in the dusty red dirt.

ON OUR SEVENTH day in Uganda, November 27th, Sharon arrives in Jinja with the FedExed letter. One miracle down! The two of us sit in the hotel dining area, waiting for Mark and Dad to return from a walk before joining us for dinner. We each order a cold drink, and I ask about her studies.

"Good. I've still got a ways to go, but I think my courses are going to really help me when I start up my project." I notice that her eyes are alight with excitement. Her future is full of possibility.

I remember Sharon's dream of starting up a children's home outside of Jinja, near her village, that specifically serves children with physical disabilities. More and more, I see that she is a gifted leader, and I have no doubt that such an organization will thrive under her guidance. The biggest hurdle, as always, will be finding funding. Yet Sharon also has an entrepreneurial spirit, which will prove to be essential as she focuses on creative ways for the orphanage to generate enough income to care for its children and workers. She asks me if I have had a chance to see Margaret yet.

"Yes. We went to visit the children's home two days ago," I reply. "It was so special to be able to show Dad where I met Mark, and for him to now be able to picture it all. I tried my best to explain things to Mark, but I'm not sure how much he understood. Most of the housemothers are all still there, and they loved seeing Mark again, of course. He looks so different now than he did when we left," I admit.

Sharon agrees that he is growing up fast. She has seen from afar how he has changed over the past few years, as I include photos of him in my emails to her. Now that I have the letter in hand, the plan is for us to depart for Mbale tomorrow. Sharon asks me if I feel ready to go.

"I'm ready for the legal stuff to all be over, for Mark and me to be able to put that part behind us," I willingly admit. I share that lately I have become a different person, my thoughts consumed with logistics and scenarios of the unknown. I feel guilty for depriving Mark of the mother he is used to having, the mother who laughed a lot more and spent her free time taking him to the waterpark or the ice rink, or danced with him to loud music, instead of briskly hauling him around from one meeting to another. *You'll get your mom back soon, Mark. Lord willing, we are almost there.*

"It is going to work out, Tandela," Sharon encourages me after letting me share all of my worries and doubts about the upcoming court date. "If you were to write down all of the miracles that God has done so far you would see that he is constantly affirming his faithfulness to you."

Just then, Mark and Dad enter the room. I watch as Sharon and Mark make eye contact.

"I can't believe how big you are now!" she exclaims to Mark with a wide smile. Dad introduces himself, and she warmly shakes his hand. "I hope this fits you," she says to Mark, holding up a t-shirt and chuckling. Sharon spends the evening with us, enjoying the questions Dad has about her studies and discussing her future plans of establishing an orphanage. It is hard to say goodbye early the next morning at the bus station.

Sharon has to be back in Kampala for a class that afternoon, and we are leaving for Mbale. Only God knows if we will ever see each other in person again. I can tell she is dwelling on similar thoughts, though she forces herself to embrace me in a cheerful hug.

"I remember when we started on this adventure." Her eyes twinkle. "I'm so glad I could be a part of it. Let me know when you learn of your court date. I will be praying for you, that God will continue to supply you with strength until you return to Canada with Mark as your son, forever."

CHAPTER FOURTEEN

November–December 2006, Uganda

T HE BUS ride to Mbale is short, and takes only two and a half hours. We go straight to the lawyer's office to learn the status of our court date. I am hoping he is going to tell us it is within the next few days.

"Mr. Moses Ugama, Attorney of Law," reads the plaque outside his office. His secretary shows us in. Sitting behind a large oak desk is Mr. Ugama — all three hundred pounds of him. His facial features are large as well. But he is not threatening, for his eyes are kind. Mark holds my hand as the three of us enter the room and climbs into my lap when I sit down. Ever since we left Canada, Mark has been uncharacteristically shy. His shyness has on occasion been mistaken as rudeness here, which is confusing for Mark. He doesn't understand why Ugandans expect him to be more talkative and outgoing. They have no idea that Mark has spent the last two-and-a half years in a totally different environment — one which assumes a lot more distance, both physically and emotionally, between strangers.

"It brings me great pleasure to finally meet you in person, Tandela." Mr. Ugama makes his way around the desk, shaking my hand first, then extending his hand to Dad. "And you, David. I am so pleased that you were able to take time from your job and join your daughter here." He leans over slowly. "And you must be Mark," he says, patting Mark softly on the head. "I trust you three had a good trip here? And that your travels have been going smoothly?"

Mr. Ugama continues to engage us in small talk before making his way back to his chair. He clasps his hands together across his belly and announces, "I could not get a court date for you here. All of the judges in Mbale are unavailable until December 15th because of a local election."

What?! What am I paying you thousands of dollars for if you can't even get us a court date? I scream in my head. Mark is the only person in the room who has not picked up on the awkwardness of the situation. He shifts himself around, trying to get comfortable on my lap. The heat is really getting to me, I still feel jet-lagged, and my patience is thinning. And now this.

"But we can try to go to Soroti," Mr. Ugama continues in a hurry, noting the look of devastation on my face. "I am optimistic I can get us a hearing in Soroti in the next ten days."

"Ten days? We don't have ten days," I state frankly. If the judge rules in our favour, after the court date we still have to travel to Nairobi to sort out Mark's immigration paperwork. A court date in ten days would be December 8th, leaving us with only ten days to get to Kenya, somehow get an appointment at the embassy, and have Mark's immigration application processed. I think it will be next to impossible to get everything done in that amount of time.

"Because after the court date we still have to go to the embassy in Kenya," I explain. "Without a permanent residency card from them, Mark is not allowed back into Canada."

"Mommy? When am I going to see Nana?" Mark blurts, sensing the tension in my voice.

"Soon, sweetie. In just a few weeks," I tell him, hoping with all of my heart that this will prove true. I will myself to stay calm and not completely lose it on Mr. Ugama. It is not his fault that there is an election that causes everything to be in flux for three weeks.

"I will do my best to get it even sooner than that," he assures me. "Hopefully December 5th or 6th."

"Is it even safe to go there?" I ask. The last time I was here, Soroti was not considered a safe place to visit because of its close proximity to the rebel activities in northern Uganda. Soroti is only one hour north of Mbale by car, but three years ago it felt like another world because of all the civil unrest there.

"Yes, things are much better there now," he says, doing his best to reassure me.

"But the farther we go from where Mark and I lived, from Jinja—won't that work against us?" I ask him.

"It would be better if you had some sort of relationship or ties to the area," Mr. Ugama agrees. "Like a local Soroti address for example. Otherwise the judge may wonder why we have traveled to a court so far from Jinja where you once lived. But I will explain everything to them. I will explain how we had no choice. And we will also have to explain this to your probation officer. Soroti is an unusually far place for him to have to travel to testify on behalf of a client."

Mr. Makiywe does not like to go out of his way for me when I am in the same city as him. I am sure he will not be happy with our request that he take an entire day off work to travel to Soroti.

TODAY IS DECEMBER 3rd. Still no court date. I am spending the afternoon with Mr. Ugama in his office signing papers while Dad and Mark explore the streets of Mbale.

"Then they will want to see this one. Sign here. And initial here. And here," he instructs me patiently.

Mr. Ugama moves slowly and deliberately. I notice a photo on his desk of his wife and their four children. His wife is tall and thin, a stark contrast to Mr. Ugama.

As we thoroughly review each document that we will present to the judge, my trust in Mr. Ugama grows. Yesterday I felt that he failed me because he did not have a court date booked for us, but this grudge is beginning to dissipate. I can accept now that the circumstances are beyond his control. If I am going to get frustrated every time that something here is not straightforward, I might as well go home right now. I can't take every misunderstanding or delay personally or I will fall apart. I need to toughen up, expect the unexpected, and be strong, for these are muddy waters I am navigating. For the last three years, the final days of the adoption process were that of the distant future, a vague concept. And now, perhaps as early as seven days from now, Mark will be legally recognized as my son.

"I wasn't able to secure a court date in Soroti for December 5th or 6th," Mr. Ugama says apologetically. "But, good news, we have one for Tuesday, December 12th."

"That's the next available date?" Despite my best attempt, there is no hiding my disappointment.

"Yes, Tandela. And after that everything is booked up for one whole week. So we are very lucky to get in on this day," he assures me, smiling with an air of sympathy.

"Our flight home is December 18th, Mr. Ugama. That gives us six days to go to Nairobi and complete the immigration process."

"Yes, well, you will probably have to change your flight. I don't think it will be at all possible for you to get the immigration work done in such a short amount of time. It usually takes months."

My confidence wanes with every word. Although we have only been in Uganda for eleven days, I feel like we have been here for weeks. My heart sags within me, making me aware of the weight I am carrying, the stress that is my constant companion. The daytime heat combined with my stress-induced insomnia has left me extremely fatigued. With every move, my limbs feel unnaturally heavy and even a small smile requires a great deal of effort. I have nine more days to wait for someone to make the biggest decision of my life.

DAD, MARK, AND I try to stay busy to help pass the time. Dad is having a wonderful trip, taking himself on random adventures each day. Yesterday he was gone when I woke up and I did not see him again until six o'clock that evening. To say he is enjoying himself is an understatement. While I spend most of my days pouring over documents and triple-checking every item in our giant dossier, Dad is having a vacation. He is not the least bit stressed or worried about this situation and is taking every opportunity to explore and soak in the culture here. Sometimes he takes Mark with him, and if not, Mark comes with me or goes and spends some time with Peter and Mary-Anne. They are still living in Mbale and have graciously invited us over for dinner a few times. Their girls are now six and eight years old and are more than happy to host a younger playmate. Mark, when given the option, always chooses to go to their house over accompanying me to Mr. Ugama's office, which he considers a bore.

Before we go to sleep every night, Dad makes sure that Mark and I have our mosquito nets properly positioned around our beds.

"Everyone in Africa should have access to these!" he declares, holding out Mark's net. "It is such a simple thing that would prevent hundreds of thousands of cases of malaria each year."

It turns out that the day before yesterday, Dad spent some time in the local hospital. The gardener at our hostel learned that he was a physician and asked Dad if he would come to the hospital with him and examine a problem he had with a disc in his back.

"I couldn't believe the number of people there waiting to see a doctor," Dad confided to me. "There are just so few nurses and doctors available to help the number of people in need." His brow furrows, the wrinkles in his forehead running deep above his concerned blue eyes.

"There you go, all set," Dad says as he finishes with Mark's net. His face relaxes as he looks at his grandson. "Good night, Mark."

"Good night, Bumpy," Mark says through his yawn. "Tomorrow we are going to the pool, right?" Mark turns to face me. I am sleeping in a single bed beside him.

"That's right, sweetie. We will go swimming tomorrow," I promise him. I am looking forward to going to the pool myself. It will be a refreshing distraction for everyone.

IT IS THIRTY-THREE degrees Celsius today, and I can think of nothing I would rather do than be near water. Mark and I hop on one boda-boda while Dad gets on another. It is refreshing to feel the wind rushing in my face as we ride. From the exterior, the pool looks like a resort — which it kind of is. It is a country club that is used mainly by expats and tourists. Anyone can pay to use the outdoor pool facilities, but the admission is too expensive for most of the locals. It looks as though every foreigner in Mbale is taking refuge from the heat here today. Mark's eyes widen with delight as we leave the change room and step onto the pool deck.

"Mommy, can I go in?" He places his hand on the railing at the shallow end and bends down, dipping one foot into the water. "It's cold!" he squeals jubilantly.

After so many days of constantly sweating from the burdensome heat, this is a wonderful treat for Mark.

I step around him and lower myself into the pool. Mark stretches out his arms and I draw him close to me. We twirl around in the water, generating ripples that carry themselves away from us in concentric circles. Mark pulls away from me and thrusts himself to the edge. He props himself up on his elbow and catches his breath.

"Mommy, look!" He lowers his face toward the water and exhales noisily, gleefully generating a cluster of tiny bubbles in the water.

His eyes shine with self-satisfaction at his own independence. For this precious hour, Mark is just a little boy in a swimming pool. Just a three-year-old enjoying the sensation of cool water instead of the scorching sun that inflames his sensitive skin. Enjoying the freedom that floating in water brings, the weightlessness and the effortlessness of it all. In the water, the two of us can just be. For a brief time, the frightening reality of the impending court decision, the immigration paperwork, and whether or not we will be able to return together to Canada drift from my mind.

Mark's breath is warm on my shoulder. He hugs me with delight as we bob up and down, up and down. He is relaxed, for he is secure in the arms of his life preserver, the one he trusts more than anyone else. The one he loves more than anyone else. I commit this moment to memory. The way drops of water rest on his wet eyelashes. The way his hair shrinks when it is wet, making him look younger than his three and a half years. The brightness of his beautiful little baby teeth when he smiles. I am his protector.

In the change room I rub his damp skin with Vaseline, hoping to keep it from drying out and cracking in the sun. The heat has caused little bumps to break out all over his body and he is scratching them constantly. I don't know if this is a reaction to heat alone or if he is actually allergic to something. We take our time getting dressed and meet Dad outside. He is deep in conversation with two boda-boda drivers. Mark and I climb on one, and Dad gets on the other. Once we are settled, our drivers slowly drive us away from the pool.

"Aaaaaaaaaahhhhhhhhh!" A horrifying wail breaks through Mark's lips as our motorcycle lurches to a stop. His head is thrown back, and he is in too much pain to even point to the source of his cries. I frantically scan Mark's body to see what is wrong and am greatly distressed to discover Mark's foot is wedged between the spokes of the motorcycle's back wheel. The white area of the wound begins to redden as it fills with blood, which then pours out onto the dusty road. Mark screams in pain. Dad rushes forward, and with nimble fingers begins to extract Mark's foot from the wheel. My arms tightly grip the rest of Mark's body, trying to hold him still as the pain increases with Dad's touch. In a matter of seconds his foot is freed. Tears continue to cascade down Mark's cheeks.

"Mark, you are going to be okay. Mommy's got you. You are going to be okay. You have to let Bumpy put this towel around your foot, okay?" I continue to make eye contact with him as Dad tightly winds one of our pool towels around Mark's foot to slow down the circulation and prevent blood loss.

"I am so sorry. I am so, so sorry," our boda-boda driver frantically apologizes. He is very upset. His eyes reveal that he is also very scared. Scared that we are going to sue him for damages.

"It's fine, it's fine," Dad reassures him. He inspects the bike's wheel, the spokes stained with blood and so misshapen from the accident that it is beyond repair. "Your bike is quite badly damaged. Here, please take this compensation." Dad piles some bills into his hand.

"No, I can't," says the driver, refusing the gesture.

"I insist. Please." Dad covers the driver's hand with his and nods.

There is a hospital two blocks away. Dad carries Mark in his arms and we walk, for there is no way Mark will get on another boda-boda today. At the hospital, Dad bandages up his foot.

"We'll have to soak it in saltwater regularly so it doesn't get infected."

I wish that our stroller had not gotten lost on the journey over, as the injury means Mark now has to be carried everywhere.

"This is not going to look good for when we go to court," I confide to Dad. "They are totally going to think I am a neglectful mother. My child can't even walk because the bandage on his foot is so big."

Dad rests his hand on my shoulder. "It will be fine," he says with a reassuring squeeze. "It's a surface wound that looks bad because it stripped away a lot of skin. We will give him some acetaminophen for the pain and keep an eye on it. Because Mark is perfectly healthy it should heal quickly." Mark's cries have subsided and he is perched on Dad's shoulders, the trauma of the accident gradually melting away as he sucks on a lollipop.

"I looked into buses," Dad continues, turning his head from Mark to meet my gaze. "We can get one out of here at eight thirty tomorrow morning. That should put us into Gulu before five."

Dad told me before we left Canada that he really wanted to visit Gulu, where the girl he and Mom are sponsoring through an organization called The Child Is Innocent lives. The organization is focused on caring for children seeking refuge and rehabilitation from the war in northern Uganda. The last thing on earth I feel like doing is take a long bus ride to visit another town. I am so exhausted. With every day the weight upon me seems to grow.

CHAPTER FIFTEEN

December 2006, Uganda

TOMORROW IS December 12th, the day we finally go to court—barring any unforeseen disaster, that is. It has been such a challenge to secure this court date that I am hesitant to fully believe it really will happen. *Something is bound to go wrong to derail this.*

We left Gulu yesterday, and from there made the three-hour trip to the town of Soroti for the court date. In Gulu, Dad was able to meet and spend time with his sponsor child, which brought him great joy. In the schools we visited, children shared personal testimonies of abductions and violence against their families. We also heard some horrifying stories from volunteers about post-traumatic stress disorder, and how they were trying to help these children who had been so thoroughly brainwashed to kill on a daily basis. I still remember the day, more than two and a half years ago, when I arrived at the children's home for my shift and learned that one of the housemothers had just received news that her family's village had been ransacked and her little brother abducted by the LRA.

In twenty years of war, nearly two million Ugandans have been displaced from their homes. The pain and suffering that has plagued these people for so many years is beyond comprehension. I hope, and a part of me believes, that with each opportunity to share their stories and be heard, a tiny bit of healing takes place. It is too late to hear their cries in the midst of the violence that the UN called "the most forgotten, worst humanitarian crisis in the world," but it is not too late to give the survivors a voice, to come alongside and help them begin again. For myself, a shift in perspective was a healthy reminder of how blessed Mark truly is.

Beep beep. I look down at my cell phone. I have a text message. It is from Mr. Makiywe. *He's probably notifying me that he's left Jinja and is on his way to Soroti,* I think to myself. Both Mr. Makiywe and Mr. Ugama are meeting us at the courthouse tomorrow morning. But I am wrong. Instead, the text says "send me $200US or I am not coming tomorrow."

Here we go. In the back of my mind I was anticipating that something was going to happen to interrupt the otherwise smooth flow of the last few days. I need Mr. Makiywe there tomorrow. Though I have his letter of support, his in-person testimony is invaluable, for he is the only one who can testify to the judge on behalf of my relationship with Mark. And now he is demanding a bribe. I stare at the text, my face flushed with anger. I am at the end of my rope with trying to satisfy everyone's needs. I never want to fill out another form or ask for another letter of reference again.

For three years I have gone beyond what has been required of me in regard to paperwork and proper documentation. For three years I have lived at the beck and call of the Ugandan and Canadian authorities, trying to satisfy their every whim so as to do everything in my power to ensure the adoption goes through. I am tired of being polite and overly cautious, making sure not to step on anyone's toes. I am tired of always going out of my way so as not to be an inconvenience to anyone.

In the eleventh hour, one day before the ruling, Mr. Makiywe threatens to jeopardize Mark and our family. How dare he use his power to blackmail me. I have been nothing but diligent and have gone above and beyond in keeping him apprised of our life in Canada. *Lord, how do I respond to him?* I sit down on the bed in our room at the hostel in Soroti. This is Mr. Makiywe's final opportunity to get some cash out of me and he knows it. If the adoption is approved tomorrow, God willing, we will probably never hear from each other again.

I recall something Peter said recently while we were over for dinner at their house about judges and probation officers being in cahoots together.

"It is not uncommon that the probation officer will pay the judge to rule favourably on a case," he said. "What happens is, even though the client is not required to pay the probation officer any money to come to court, the probation officer demands he be paid a certain amount of cash and he then gives the judge a cut of these funds in exchange for a favourable ruling."

Is this what is going on with Mr. Makiywe? Is he planning on splitting the two hundred dollars with the judge? If so, it will be of no use to explain to the judge tomorrow why Mr. Makiywe has refused to come. The judge will dislike me even more for refusing to pay, for it means he will have lost out on a chance to make some easy cash. On the other hand, Jinja is quite a distance from Soroti. Mr. Makiywe knows all the judges in Jinja and a number in Kampala and perhaps even Mbale, but Soroti is over two hundred kilometres from Jinja. I doubt that Mr. Makiywe has spent much time in Soroti; therefore, it's less likely that he knows many judges here. In fact, I am not even sure if Mr. Makiywe has ever traveled to Soroti at all for a court date. Considering that only three years ago Soroti was an unsafe place to be with all of the rebel activity here, it definitely would not have been a popular destination for adoption hearings.

I squeeze my hands together, yearning to hear God's voice, longing for some wisdom and discernment. I pull out my list of four Bible verses that I wrote out before I left for Uganda. I chose specific verses to encourage me through difficult moments, and now is a time when I need to be encouraged. I read the top one:

You will not have to fight this battle. Take up your positions; stand firm and see the deliverance the LORD will give you, Judah and

Jerusalem. Do not be afraid; do not be discouraged. Go out to face them tomorrow, and the LORD will be with you.

(2 Chronicles 20:17)

"You will not have to fight this battle... Do not be afraid; do not be discouraged... the Lord will be with you," I repeat out loud. God has always made a way for things to come to pass without relying on corrupt methods. He will not fail me now. My conscience clear, my hands calm, I text Mr. Makiywe: "No, Mr. Makiywe. If you are not here tomorrow, I will tell the judge why you are a no-show."

If Mr. Makiywe is not in cahoots with the judge, and our judge disdains such corrupt practices, it will be in Mr. Makiywe's best interest to keep this request between him and me.

I STRETCH MY legs and try to ease the tension in my body by leaning against the pillar outside our hostel dormitory. The grounds are softly lit by a gleaming sliver of moon. The air is still and quiet, save for the occasional bird call. Dad is reading, huddled close to the lone lamp in our room, while Mark, already in a deep sleep, lies in the bed next to him.

I have not heard back from Mr. Makiywe. There is little to make me believe he will show up at the courthouse tomorrow. I am scared of what tomorrow may bring. I feel my body shutting down. Is this how a breakdown begins? My hands are shaking and tears begin streaming down my cheeks. The stress has finally broken me. *God, I am so scared.*

In the past, I have been able to bury this fear in doing something, in filling out some form or writing some letter. But now there is nothing left for me to do. Nothing. We have come so far and the judge can still say no. And Mark will be taken away from me. There will be no appeal. There is no such thing as an appeal process here. Mark could be taken without an explanation of his whereabouts and Ugandan authorities can force me out of the country.

I go inside and try to lie down, lie still, even if I cannot sleep.

Have I made his life worse, Lord? I think I might throw up. I am sick with the thought that for almost three years I have exposed Mark to a family and a life that he will never see again. As a three-year-old, he will be forced to leave the only culture, the only language he has ever known. He will go from having a large family that loves him to being sent to an orphanage where he knows no one. *Lord, may the judge have mercy on us,* I pray. *May he look favourably on our case.*

My aching heart can't help but dwell on possible scenarios. What if the judge tomorrow is corrupt? What if our judge has had horrible experiences with Westerners? What if he uses the fact that I fostered Mark in Canada rather than Uganda against me? Or argues that I am an illegitimate parent because I am single? And not of the same sex as Mark as is required by Ugandan law? I try to lay these fears at God's feet and give them up to him instead of being paralyzed by fear. *Lord, forgive me for my doubts.* I repeat over and over a passage from the Psalms. I have committed these verses to memory, for it is one of the specific passages I wrote out before leaving for Uganda:

May he give you the desire of your heart
    and make all your plans succeed.
May we shout for joy over your victory
    and lift up our banners in the name of our God.
May the LORD grant all your requests.

(Psalm 20:4-5)

Oh God, hear me. Grant this request. I desperately want to shout for joy tomorrow.

I don't remember falling asleep. But I must have at some point, because the next thing I remember is reaching for my phone and checking the time. 4:45 a.m., Tuesday, December 12th.

Today is the day.

THE HEARING IS in an hour and a half and I still have not heard a thing from Mr. Makiywe.

"Dad, we should get going," I say, stuffing a couple of Mark's books into my bag.

"Mommy, my shoe. Can you help me?" Mark holds up his sandal.

"Sure, Mark. Sit down on the bed here and I'll do it up."

The wound on Mark's foot is improving daily, and now that he is able to bear weight on it he can walk around, albeit with a slight limp. However, he still wears a large bandage, and so it is difficult for him to secure his sandal straps on his own.

Outside, Dad waves down two boda-bodas. The ride to the courthouse is short. The building resembles the High Court in Jinja, which is to say that it looks more like a motel than a courthouse. After all of the drama we have gone through to get here, it feels a bit anti-climactic to have the final showdown at such a nondescript building. Three guards are stationed near the entrance. As we approach the main doors, we pass a man who is being escorted out. His hands are bound in chains. I wonder what his morning has been like. Has he just received a sentence? To my great relief, I find Mr. Ugama *and* Mr. Makiywe sitting in the waiting area.

"I have notified them that we are here," Mr. Ugama informs me. At eleven o'clock, an hour and a half after our appointment time, a clerk informs us that the judge will now see us in his chambers. We follow the clerk to the door of the chambers and he motions for us to stop.

"You will go in and sit down," he instructs the five of us. "You will not make eye contact with the judge and you will not speak to him unless you are spoken to. If you are spoken to then you must stand and address the judge as 'my Lord.'"

I try my best not to smirk. *My Lord?* This is too much. No one on earth deserves such a title. I hope that I will not have to address the judge. I don't think I could do it.

The chambers resemble a typical big office. The judge, a large man adorned in a dark green robe, sits behind a desk facing a row of chairs. He instructs us to sit down. Mr. Makiywe, Dad, and I sit in a row of chairs facing the judge, while Mr. Ugama takes a seat closer to the judge's desk in one of two chairs reserved for attorneys. As usual, Mark sits in my lap. I place my hands as naturally as possible over Mark's left foot, trying to hide the large bandage on his heel. Mr. Makiywe has given me strict instructions not to let Mark move or make any noise. How am I supposed to do that? Three-year-olds don't like to sit still and be quiet.

"I now commence the hearing for the client of Mr. Moses Ugama, the day of December 12th, 2006. Mr. Ugama, please rise and state your case," the judge commands.

"My Lord," Mr. Ugama begins, "I am presenting you with this petition."

I know the petition by heart, I have read it so many times. It contains fourteen points and an extensive appendix.

"My Lord, this young woman from Canada wants to adopt this boy," Mr. Ugama gestures to Mark, who is sitting in my lap and twirling my hair in his fingers as he silently takes in his surroundings. "She has had him in her home for three years. As you can see, my Lord, he is very attached to her."

Mr. Ugama gingerly places the petition along with the additional thirteen appendices on the judge's desk.

The judge raises his eyebrows and his eyes widen as he takes in the giant stack of paperwork in front of him. Mr. Ugama mailed our entire dossier to the courthouse in advance of our appointment, but the expression on the judge's face suggests this is the first time he has laid eyes on it.

"I have included all of the supporting documents in this petition, my Lord, including a booklet explaining the adoption laws that pertain to the province in Canada where Tandela is living so as to provide you with assurance that we have abided by the laws there. If you would be so kind as to peruse these documents, it would be very much appreciated. I am sorry we are taking so much of your time, my Lord," Mr. Ugama adds apologetically.

Silence ensues. The judge adjusts his glasses and scans the first page of the petition, then the second. He pushes the entire dossier to the side of his desk, claps his hands together, and leans forward.

"There is a lot of concern around child trafficking," he says sternly. "We have to be very particular about who we grant adoptions to. It seems the latest trend is for white people to adopt black babies. Why is this? Everyone wants to be like Madonna. And now Angelina Jolie. And you think that you deserve special privileges, that you don't have to abide by our policies or our laws. We have systems in place for a reason. Do not expect me to give you special treatment because you are white," he emphasizes loudly. "These are my chambers and this is *my* decision. I will *not* be swayed by your speeches."

I tighten my arms around Mark's waist. *Lord, don't let Mark be taken away.* Adrenaline is pulsing through my body. I want to run and take Mark with me. Run to a place where the judge will never find us, to a place where we will be safe and together.

"I can see that he is very attached to you." The sudden softening of the judge's demeanour brings forth a rush of hope inside me. "What do you have to say in respect to Ms. Swann's adoption request?" He directs this question to Mr. Makiywe, the man who is probably still ticked off at me for not paying him to come here.

Mr. Makiywe stands and clears his throat.

"My Lord, I have never met someone in all of the world who is as loving and caring as Tandela. She has a beautiful heart, my Lord."

I cannot believe what I am hearing. It sounds like a Hallmark card. Mr. Makiywe has a tendency to be overly dramatic, and apparently today he is holding nothing back.

"This young woman mothered this child and brought him up from the dust. She is his saviour, this young girl helping her fellow man. And they have a wonderful life together. A life better than all the riches in the world. If only our fellow men would help one another, things would be much better and different here. We must work for the common good, all of us. And I believe that if we do, then the moon and the sun and the stars —"

"Thank you, I think we have heard enough," the judge interrupts, cutting Mr. Makiywe off from some random poetic tangent about the greater good. *How is any of what he said helpful to our case?* Mr. Makiywe said nothing about all the letters he received from us while we were in Canada, nothing about my character or my relationship with Mark or how good his health is. Really, he said nothing concrete at all in his bizarre speech.

"You are going to have to give me a week to review all of this material," the judge announces. I hope he is saying that in jest. We have a flight booked to Kenya the day after tomorrow to get Mark's immigration paperwork finished.

The judge stands up and motions toward the door. "Thank you and come back in a week."

Oh no. He is dead serious.

"A week! Dad, you know we can't wait here for another week," I say in a panicked voice outside the chambers. I send a pleading look to Mr. Ugama, who shrugs his shoulders in response.

"Moses, is there anything that can be done?" Dad asks. "Can we ask him to review it quicker?"

"No, no," Mr. Ugama cautions us. "We are out of his chambers now. He has made his decision. We want him to look favourably on us. We cannot go back in there and speak with him. These things are not done. It is unheard of."

"But our flights," I say. "We will have to change our flights and who knows how much that will cost and…" I trail off. That will put us in Kenya around December 21st, and the embassy will surely be closed for Christmas holidays. I will have to wait until January to even inquire after Mark's application. Dad will head home alone, and Mark and I will be left here over Christmas, desperately hoping that when we show up at the embassy in January we will not be forced to wait weeks or even months for Mark to be issued a permanent residence card. Before I say another word, Dad puts his hand on the door of the chambers and waltzes in as if he has just received an invitation from the judge himself.

"Excuse me, my Lord," he begins. "I don't know if this is at all possible, but we have flights booked for the day after tomorrow to Kenya, so if there is any way for you to maybe consider reviewing the paperwork a little bit quicker we would be incredibly grateful." I peer through the door to see if the judge is going to explode at the boldness of this tall, lanky white man standing before him.

"I see," the judge begins, glancing at Dad, then me, and then Mark. "Well then, come back tomorrow morning and we will see."

My body is flooded with the sensation of relief. Tomorrow. That is not as good as getting the green light today, but it is a thousand times better than having to wait another week. I hold my excitement in, forcing myself to look emotionless but nevertheless walking quickly toward the exit. Mark holds fast to my hand and his walk turns into a skip as he struggles to keep up while favouring his good foot.

"Dad, I can't believe you just did that!" I exclaim as the heavy courthouse door closes behind us.

"Tandy, I've been around enough to know that if people understand the circumstances, they will often make adjustments," Dad calmly explains.

"But weren't you nervous going back in there?"

"Of course I was nervous," Dad admits. "I don't know how the system works here. But the judge didn't know how big an inconvenience one week would be for us. You don't always have to accept what you are told," he reminds me. "There is often another way."

I am so glad my dad is here. There is no way I would have done what he did.

"You owe me money, Tandela," Mr. Makiywe announces. "I need you to pay me something for all this," he says, gesturing toward the courthouse.

"What are you talking about? This is your job," I respond. Is he trying to blackmail me again?

"It is my job to come to court when it is in my jurisdiction. That is Jinja. But for this, I had to travel. So you need to give me some money for my expenses."

"That is reasonable," I agree. "We will pay for your travel expenses and your lodging."

"Thank you. That will be two hundred and fifty dollars."

I laugh at the absurdity of the request.

"No, it will not be!"

Soroti is not exactly a hot tourist destination, and there are no expensive hotels here. An average overnight stay would cost between fifteen and twenty dollars. To take the bus up here from Jinja would have cost Mr. Makiywe ten dollars.

"What? How do you know what I spent? I am telling you I need two hundred and fifty."

"Okay, give me your receipts and I will reimburse you," I reply, confident Mr. Makiywe has not found a way to spend over two hundred dollars for two nights' accommodation.

"We have no problem paying you what you need to be paid," Dad says gently, trying to pacify the situation. "We just want to make sure that we are being above reproach in all of this. That is why it would be helpful for you to present your receipts. Then everything will be organized and documented," he adds.

"Receipts?!" Mr. Makiywe bursts out. "You think I keep receipts? I never keep receipts. Why would I do that? You did not tell me I needed to. I do not have a receipt from my bus here, and I do not have a receipt from the hotel last night. I have told you what I need and you do not believe me. Go to the hotel. Ask them what it costs. You will see!"

His face is darkening, reddening. He is intent on squeezing some last cash out of us and we are not responding according to his plan. "I think I will go right back into the judge's chambers and tell him I take back everything I said about you. I will tell him it is not true, that you are not a good mother," he spits, his eyes locked onto mine.

I know Mr. Makiywe well enough by now to recognize that this is likely an empty threat, for such behaviour would cause him to look foolish in front of the judge. No longer do I have to walk on eggshells around Mr. Makiywe, revering him because of his authoritative position. I am finally free from having to bend over backward so that he will be willing to provide his signature to support our cause.

"Fine, go ahead," I say, shrugging.

"Just give him what he wants," Mr. Ugama pleads in an effort to mediate the situation. We are making quite the scene outside of the courthouse. "It is not very much money to you."

"It is not about the money. I don't care about the amount. I care about not paying bribes for Mark. He is a person. I am not buying him. I am asking the government permission to adopt him. There is a difference. Like the judge said, there are systems in place for this sort of thing. I am just trying to do everything according to the system here."

"I am not asking for a bribe, Tandela. I am asking for money so I can eat some food and sleep at night!

I have no receipts, you have to believe I am telling the truth." He looks into my eyes earnestly for what is probably the first and last time.

Remembering my conversation with Naomi, I weigh her words against Mr. Makiywe's request.

"I will reimburse you," I relent, and quickly determine an amount I think is reasonable. "I will give you seventy-five dollars." I dig into my purse and pull out my wallet.

"Thank you." Mr. Makiywe tucks the bills in his pocket. "This is not enough, but I will make do." He throws his shoulders back and looks down at me. "Goodbye, Tandela."

I stare blankly at him, unsure of what to say as his role in this journey comes to a close. "Goodbye, Mr. Makiywe. Thank you for everything."

He lingers as though there is something he wants to say. Everyone is quiet, waiting. He nods, takes one step backward, then turns and walks away. I watch him disappear behind the compound walls.

And that is the last time I ever see Mr. Makiywe.

Switching back into business mode, I tell Dad I have to go straight to an internet café. "I told Andrea, the manager of Alberta Adoption Services, our hearing was today so that if the adoption was granted she would be prepared to receive a fax of the official letter. We need that letter from her to push Mark's paperwork through at the embassy. I have to tell her that tomorrow will hopefully be the day."

If the adoption goes through, tomorrow is going to be a crazy day. In order for us to get the letter from Andrea before we leave on the bus to Kampala in the late afternoon, she is going to have to be at work early tomorrow morning, before seven o'clock. And we must have this document from Andrea to complete Mark's paperwork at the embassy in Nairobi. Since Uganda is nine hours ahead, it means that we cannot expect to receive her fax until around four o'clock tomorrow afternoon. I am hoping we will make the last bus to Kampala. There is no schedule—the bus will leave Soroti when it is full.

I notify Andrea of our change in timeline and write a quick email to friends and family back home, asking for prayer for all of the little things that have to line up in order for us to receive the adoption order and make it to Kampala tomorrow night.

"Tandy, you have to eat something. You've hardly eaten in days," Dad urges me. We choose to eat dinner in the dimly lit hotel restaurant. Even the most basic hotels in Uganda have kitchens that are always on standby for whoever happens to wander in. We are the only ones in the room. I have ordered a plate of rice and beans for Mark and me to share, knowing I will hardly touch any myself. I cannot remember the last time I felt hungry.

"I'm fine, Dad. Stop worrying about me." I am short with him. I have no more patience. How can he be so relaxed? Doesn't he know the significance of what tomorrow can bring? Every day is a new adventure for him, and for me, every day brings more stress. How can he be so carefree? Sensing my mood, Dad looks out the window.

"It is a beautiful evening and it's finally cooled down a bit. I'm going to go for a walk. Want to join me, Mark?"

"Yes, Bumpy! Can I go on your shoulders?"

"You sure can. Come on, let's enjoy our last night in Soroti and give your mom some time to rest." He winks over his shoulder as they turn to leave.

As much as I find Dad's relaxed demeanour frustrating, I am grateful for the extra set of hands to attend to Mark. I am mad at myself because I have not had as much patience with Mark as usual. And it is not his fault. He has been so good here. Ferried around to one appointment after another in the sweltering heat that aggravates his skin, eating different foods, and — above all — the confusion he has faced because while he physically looks like a local, he is as out of place culturally as Dad and I are.

Hours later, I lay on my bed, listening to Mark's heavy breathing. His sleeping posture is as it was when I met him years ago, his mouth slightly gaping open and his hands nestled under his chin. Mark's teddy bear lies inches from his face, having been released from his grasp when he relaxed into a deep sleep. Dad is fast asleep, too, even though he only put down his book minutes ago. I thought that it was all going to be over by tonight. And yet the agony has only been postponed. *I can't take any more suspense.* But I am too fatigued to cry, and too tired to fall asleep.

CHAPTER SIXTEEN

December 2006, Uganda & Kenya

I **HAVE NOW** gone forty-eight hours with hardly any rest. Our bags are packed. Once we leave the hostel today, if all goes well, we will not return. I try not to think of the various scenarios that would force me to come back here. I feel dizzy as I ride on the boda-boda with Mark to the courthouse. I don't know if this is because I haven't eaten regularly or if it is my nerves. Nothing seems clear, nothing seems real. It is as though I have stepped outside of myself and am watching from a distance, waiting to see what is going to happen.

343

We wait for two hours in the main foyer of the Soroti High Court. For two hours I sit, hardly moving. For once, a million thoughts do not compete for attention in my mind; instead, my brain feels like it has gone to mush. In my dazed state, I notice a clerk walking toward us. The scene unfolds before me as if in slow motion. The clerk eventually reaches my side and extends his hand. One piece of paper hangs limp in his grasp. In a conscious effort, I lift my trembling hands to take the paper. Shivers race up my spine as I gaze at the document.

On reading the petition of Tandela Lynne Swann and the affidavit of Tandela Lynne Swann and the exhibits annexed to them and on hearing Mr. Moses Ugama Counsel for the Petitioner.

And the court being satisfied that the declarations contained in the petition are true, and being also satisfied with the undertakings of Tandela Lynne Swann the petitioner as to the care and protection and other provisions to be made for the child Mark Kirab Swann that he could be adopted by the petitioner Tandela Lynne Swann and that all the requirements of the Children Act have been complied with.

It is ordered that Tandela Lynne Swann the Petitioner be authorized to adopt the child Mark Kirab Swann.

And it is directed that the Registrar of Births and Deaths shall make entry recording this adoption in the Adopted Children Registrar in the form set out in Form H. And it is further directed that the Registrar of Births and Deaths shall cause the birth entry to be marked with the word "adopted" and shall include the above date of birth in the entry recording the adoption as provided in Form H.

"We got it," I manage to say aloud. I am numb with shock.

"It was approved?" Dad asks, his eyes wide and beginning to fill with tears.

"What does it say, Mommy?" Mark asks, curious.

"It says that you are officially my son and I am officially your Mommy. Nobody can take that from us now, buddy." I lean down and give him a kiss on the cheek.

My Mark. My son. I feel like a switch has turned me back on and I can think again. Everything has settled back into focus and my mind is racing toward all that has to be accomplished so Mark and I can return to Canada in five days. I can't quite compute that the adoption has been legalized by the Ugandan government. Perhaps I am not fully convinced that this part is over. All I know for sure is that there is still another big hoop to jump through before I can bring Mark home. I glance at my watch. It is four fifteen in the morning in Calgary.

"We should get going. We have to get this information to Canada so they can issue us the letter we need for Mark's immigration application."

We take boda-bodas to the closest internet café. In my pocket is the fax number to the Ministry of Alberta Children's Services. I address the cover page to Andrea and fax in the letter. I wait an agonizing two minutes before the machine signals that the fax has gone through. I call her direct line and leave a message on her voicemail.

"Well, I guess we've got a couple of hours to kill," I anxiously admit to Mark and Dad.

"Good, good. What shall we do now? Shall we go for a walk? Do you feel like doing some exploring, Mark?"

"Dad! Are you kidding? You can't afford to get lost somewhere. We have to catch the bus to Entebbe, and we have no idea when the last bus leaves. We can't go exploring. We have to stay focused," I urge him.

"Mom, I'm hungry," Mark tugs on my hand.

"Okay. Let's find a place to have a snack while we wait for the fax. They don't serve food here."

Mark holds my hand and limps outside. As we step out into the blazing sunlight it sinks in that a Ugandan judge has declared that I am legally, forever, Mark's mother. It is finished. There is nothing that can change that, nothing that can alter the status of Mark being my beloved son. His little hand tucked inside mine brings a flashback of three years ago. The two of us are in Jinja outside of our home early one morning. Mark is sitting on the ground, and we are holding hands and swinging our arms together, back and forth, back and forth, with glee.

I can hardly remember my life before I met him. Mark has changed me. Mark has helped me understand more about who God is and the true meaning behind Scripture verses that declare we are God's children. The Apostle John, the one who writes most about love, penned the words:

Yet to all who did receive him, to those who believed in his name, he gave the right to become children of God—children born not of natural descent, nor of human decision or a husband's will, but born of God.

(John 1:12-13)

Our standing as God's children does not come from our skin colour or our ethnicity. It is not based on genetics nor is it inherited from parents. And it does not come from our own will. It is not a choice we make; it is not something that happens because we want it to. Instead, it is like adoption. It happens because of who God our Father is and the choice that he has made to make us his children. God "predestined us for adoption to sonship through Jesus Christ, in accordance with his pleasure and will" (Ephesians 1:5).

This journey with Mark has helped me see that earthly adoption is the greatest reflection of what it means to have God say, *Receive me as your parent because I have chosen you. Receive me, the one who created you, and believe in me.* Mark's claim that he is my son will not be based on how much he looks like me but on the legal papers that bind us together, for these papers contain a promise. There is nothing Mark can do to lose this status.

"Wait. Dad, take a photo of us." I hand Dad our little point-and-shoot camera and root through the blue folder where I carefully placed the judge's letter. In one hand I hold up the letter, and in the other arm I hold Mark. Dad snaps the photo, ensuring that this memory secures a place in our scrapbook.

But my human heart cannot help but dwell on the what-ifs. All I can think of is whether or not we will get the fax we need in time to catch the bus. It is as though my body is refusing to completely let it all sink in until I have Mark's permanent residency card in my hands.

Mark has some juice and a piece of toast at a nearby restaurant. I still have no appetite. I try to be patient and not rush Mark through his food, to shield him from my nervous energy. It will be better for everybody if he stays relaxed.

We return to the internet café two hours later.

"For you!" The young woman who staffs the internet café is waving my fax from Canada. Fluttering in her hand, as though it is nothing more than scrap paper, is the last piece of the puzzle to my three-year adoption quest.

"Thank you," I cry breathlessly as I rush up to the counter. Across the top is written "Letter of No Involvement." These words attest to the fact that the Canadian government has had no involvement in arranging the adoption (legally it cannot because Uganda has not ratified the Hague Adoption Convention), but that it is recognizing the adoption on the grounds that it has been finalized in the birth country of the child. The letter states:

Section 73 of the Alberta Child, Youth and Family Enhancement Act states "An adoption effected according to the law of any jurisdiction outside Alberta has the effect in Alberta of an adoption made under this Act, if the effect of the adoption order in the other jurisdiction is to create a permanent parent-child relationship."

I quickly scan the rest of the letter, stopping to pause at the section that refers to Mark's immigration:

...we ask that Canada Immigration confirm prior to issuing the record of Landing (Form 1000) that this document is confirmation of an adoption order and that it has the same effect as an adoption granted in Alberta.

I am confident that this letter will satisfy any concerns the immigration office in Kenya may have. I place it in an envelope along with this morning's letter, ensuring they are both secure and well-protected in my blue plastic folder. Then I swing Mark up into my arms, sharing my joy.

WE FIND OURSELVES once again at the muddy field where all the buses pass through Soroti Park. We locate the one heading for Kampala, pay our fares, and wait. The bus is about two-thirds full. We are able to find three seats together toward the back. Over the next hour, more passengers filter in. Once all the seats on either side are taken, the driver brings out seats that fit down the middle aisle, which means once you are in, it is very difficult to get out. This is when Dad and Mark decide they need to use the bathroom.

"I'll climb to the front and you hoist Mark to me through the window," Dad suggests.

"You couldn't have gone earlier?" I say in disbelief.

I watch Dad awkwardly make his way toward the door, interrupting everyone in the middle aisle as he went. As if we didn't already stand out enough!

"Here, a little lower, yes. I've got you, Mark," Dad says reassuringly. I make sure Mark's left foot does not get banged up as he exits the bus through a window like an escape artist. I can tell from his smile that this is the highlight of his day.

"Be quick; we don't know when the bus might leave," I urge them. About five minutes after they wander out of sight the driver turns on the ignition. *Oh dear. Where is Dad? Why did he pick now of all times to wander off?* The driver puts his foot to the pedal and the wheels begin to turn over the reddish brown dirt. We start to gain speed. *I have to do something.* I stand up in my seat and prepare to make a scene. I have no choice but to somehow stop this bus. As I open my mouth, the sight of Dad running with Mark in his arms whirls into view.

"Stop!" Dad waves a free hand frantically. "Wait! Please!"

"Thank you, thank you so much," Dad pants as the front door swings open. He manages to awkwardly manoeuvre himself and Mark down the overcrowded aisle.

Grinning, Dad plops down in the seat next to me with Mark, who is giggling uncontrollably.

"Well, that was fun. Always good to have a little exercise before a long trip to stretch the legs. I feel much better now."

WHERE AM I? My face is soaking wet. Someone is sobbing uncontrollably. I realize suddenly that it is me. I cannot stop. I remember now. It is late at night on Wednesday, December 13th. Earlier this morning in Soroti we learned the adoption had gone through, and now we are in Kampala, sleeping at a guest house before we catch our flight to Kenya tomorrow. My body heaves as the sobs crash through me, one wave after another. Each cry unleashes a little more of the anxiety that I have buried deep within me. Day after day, year after year. It is as though my body is purging itself, cleansing itself, saying, "We don't need this anymore. The adoption has gone through. There is no need to carry this burden."

It is finished. *Was it a dream? Did it really happen?* I reach down beside my bed. My fingers run over the plastic blue folder. I pull it onto the bed. *Is the letter there?* I check. Both letters are there. *It really happened.* I put the folder down. I pick it up again. I need to double-check. I am scared. *It was a dream, just a dream,* I hear a voice whisper. I check again. The letters are there. Am I losing my mind? *Thank you, God. Thank you, God. You are so good.* Mark is in a bed next to me, sound asleep, curled on his side. I watch his back move under the covers, with each breath. Up and down. My son. Forever.

How could I have doubted you so many times, Lord? Thank you for your faithfulness. I let my body do what it needs to do, and I cry until there is nothing left.

THE NEXT DAY we fly to Nairobi, arriving in the late afternoon. It is too late to go to the High Commission of Canada office, so our plan is to be there as soon as it opens the following morning. Tomorrow is Friday. The immigration section of the High Commission is closed on the weekend, and we leave Monday at six o'clock in the evening. That means everything needs to happen tomorrow. Ideally, it was never going to be this rushed, but the delayed court date set us back.

"It should all be straightforward," I say with certainty to Dad while en route to the office early Friday morning. "I checked my email last night and Andrea Sutherland said she faxed the letter of no involvement to the immigration section of the High Commission office, which means the application is complete. I don't see why it would take more than an hour or so. Then we can finally relax this weekend."

Mark leans against me in the back seat of the taxi and rubs his eyes, tired from all the travel of the past few days in addition to the early wake-up call this morning. I lift my head to glimpse my reflection in the taxi's review mirror. My eyelids are puffy and there are grey shadows under my eyes. My normally full cheeks sit sunken in my face even with my best efforts to brighten them with blush. This probably has to do with my barely eating over the last two weeks. I cannot wait until this is all over and done with, until I have Mark's permanent residency card in my hand.

Thankfully, this is now the easy part. We are no longer at the mercy of a judge's emotions or a probation officer's greed. Getting Mark's permanent residence card does not depend on pleasing a particular authority, it depends on having compiled all the necessary paperwork. Which we have. There is no reason for me to be anxious anymore.

We show our passports to the guard at the booth and he buzzes us in the main doors. The security setup is more advanced than when I was here three years ago. Once we have cleared security, we are faced with two signs. One directs us toward the High Commission's consular services. "For Canadian Citizens Only," the sign reads. The consular section is technically considered Canadian soil, and it provides services only for Canadian citizens, as well as luxurious amenities such as computer workstations, tennis courts, and a swimming pool. The other sign directs us toward the immigration section. Africans who want to travel to Canada have to go to this section to apply for a visa. Since Mark is a Ugandan citizen, this is where we need to go.

We follow the sign down a narrow hallway and come face to face with a large glass wall. It is the entrance to immigration, but the front door is locked and inside all the lights are off. It is closed.

"That's weird. Did they shut down this office? Maybe they are doing everything out of the consulate now," I suggest. "I guess we have to head there instead."

Back we go to where the departments converge, and this time we follow the sign to the consulate section. Outside the main doors is a guard who is in charge of checking passports. With Mark's passport I include the adoption approval letter from the judge in Soroti. He waves us in. I immediately approach the front desk.

"Excuse me," I begin, "I need to speak with someone about a permanent residency application that I have filed here."

"That would be with immigration," the clerk replies.

"Yes, immigration," I agree. "So can we speak to someone about this immigration application?"

"No, *immigration*," the clerk says emphatically. "Immigration is there." He points back toward where we have just come from. "It is closed today," he adds.

"But I have to speak with someone today," I plead. "I have to fly back to Canada on Monday and my son needs his permanent residence card. All the paperwork is here. It's probably already been approved. I just need the actual card. That's all."

"I cannot help you. This section is for matters

concerning Canadian citizens only. There is nothing I can do for someone who does not have a Canadian passport."

"But can you call someone?" This cannot be happening. I will not let this happen. We have to see someone today.

"I am sorry, Miss, there is nothing I can do. We are totally different departments; we have no access and no communication with them. I suggest you come back when they open on Monday." I can feel tears welling up. I can't handle this. This was supposed to be the easy part.

"Come on, Tandy," Dad says, putting his arm around my shoulder. "There is nothing more we can do."

I sit dejected at one of the computer stations. While I'm here I might as well write Mom and Kirsten. They'll be wondering how things went today. I type "right down to the wire" in the subject line, and fill them in that we won't know until Monday whether or not Mark will be granted residency in Canada. I give them my new cell phone number, as I had to buy a new SIM card for my phone when we arrived in Kenya. I force myself to end the email on a hopeful note and write, "Love you! Believing that we will see you soon!"

IN AN ATTEMPT to distract me from the situation at hand and occupy Mark, Dad takes charge and fills our weekend with tourist activities, including spending Saturday at a wildlife reserve. When we arrived in Nairobi on Friday morning, we hailed a car at the airport and found ourselves a wonderful driver, whom we ended up hiring for the weekend. He is taking good care of us, and on Sunday he took us to his church and an afternoon barbecue hosted by a family member. Just as important, he is punctual and reliable and understands the seriousness of our situation. At seven thirty Monday morning he drops us off at the High Commission gates.

"I will wait here for you," he promises us.

"I HAVE NO record of this application," the visa officer informs me.

"It's here. It has to be here. I sent it in six months ago." I am unsuccessful at keeping my voice steady. It takes all the self-control I have not to jump over the desk and demand to look for the application myself.

"I have looked through the entire pile of applications for Canadian PR cards. We do not have your paperwork and no one here recalls seeing the application that you describe. If you would like to resubmit

I can give you the forms or you can use one of our computers in the consulate area," he patiently explains. "And you will have to gather again all the supporting documents for the application. When you are done, come back and see me and we will see what we can do. Maybe we can even get it done in less than three months. That is all I can do for you." He shrugs his shoulders as a final statement to my defeat.

I am mindful that in less than seven hours we are supposed to check in for our flights. *You do not have time to fall apart,* I tell myself. If I am going to accomplish anything I have to stay level-headed while doing it. The situation necessitates I remain calm and think clearly.

"Mark, come with me, buddy."

I take his hand, and we walk back down the hall to the consulate area. I fill Dad in on the situation along the way. From within the blue folder that contains all my precious documents, I pull out a paper with the business number of James Sheraton, the lawyer whose firm was responsible for mailing the application to the Case Processing Centre in Mississauga. From there, the application should have been mailed directly to Nairobi. It is two o'clock in the morning in Calgary. I leave a message on the office voicemail. Maybe someone will come in to the office early and get my message. I hold James's cell number in my hand. I don't want to call him in the middle of the night, but I do not know what else to do. I dial the number. It rings four times and goes to voicemail. I leave another message.

"Maybe you will only have to stay here a few weeks," Dad says, a hopeful look in his eyes. Barring a miracle, Dad is going to get on his plane later today, and Mark and I will be left here to start his residency application from scratch. It is now eleven thirty. We have three and a half hours before we have to leave for the airport. I stare at the front doors of the consulate, trying to think of what else I can do. Where could the application be? I observe a Caucasian man stroll in, dressed head to toe in khaki as though he is on his way to a safari. He looks to be in his late fifties. He walks with purpose toward the area reserved for consulate staff. Dad and I both have the same thought at the same time. *He must work here.*

"Excuse me!" Dad calls out loudly. He rushes over to the man. "Hello there, hi, perhaps you can help us," Dad says, his politeness tinged with desperation. "We've run into a bit of a problem, my daughter, grandson, and I. We sent in paperwork for my grandson's permanent residency card six months ago and have come to pick it up today only to learn that they can't find it and have told us we have to start the entire process again. And since our flights leave tonight at six o'clock, that is quite devastating news for us. And I just thought maybe if you worked here you may be able to help us..." Dad trails off.

"I do work here," the man replies, a slightly amused expression on his face. "I am the Canadian High Commissioner."

He studies Mark, then looks up at me and back down at his watch. His demeanour shifts back into business mode. "Wait here. I'll see what I can do."

He returns twenty minutes later. "I have someone looking into it," he says. "Just hang around and see what happens. I think it will be okay." He glances again at his watch. "You know," he pauses, "you have incredible timing. I wasn't supposed to be here today. I am leaving the country myself in a few hours for a vacation. It was only because I realized this morning I forgot my glasses in my office that I came by. Makes you think, now, doesn't it?" He smiles and pats Mark on the head. "Have a good trip home, son."

One hour later the visa officer that we had dealt with on the immigration side sheepishly informs us that the application has been located "in the bottom of some pile," and they have also found Andrea's fax. "See, it has all worked out." The officer forces a laugh. But I don't find it the least bit funny. Maybe ten years down the road I will laugh about this. Not today. But still I pause to thank God. *Thank you, God, for sending that kind man when you did and for retrieving our carelessly placed application.*

"Come back in a couple of hours." The officer instructs us. "It will take us a couple of hours to process and then it will be done. Go have lunch, and return by four p.m."

Two hours. In two hours we will have the visa. In two hours we should have already checked in at the airport. This is cutting it really close.

"Okay, thank you. Our flight leaves at six tonight. Is there any way we can get it sooner?"

"Six?" the clerk repeats. "You'll have plenty of time. We'll have it here for you by four. That is lots of time."

Good grief. *No*, I want to argue. It takes well over half an hour to get to the airport from here, and we will be driving at rush hour, and we are supposed to check in no less than two hours before our flight, so *no*, that does not give us lots of time.

"Okay, Mark, let's go get something to eat. Are you looking forward to getting on a plane today?"

"Am I going to get a window seat?" Mark asks hopefully.

"We'll ask when we check in. Maybe," Dad smiles like he knows a secret, and Mark smiles back.

True to his word, our driver is waiting for us outside.

"We have to come back in two hours," I explain. "They say it will be ready then. But I don't know how we are going to get to the airport in time. We will have barely an hour to check in and get through security before the gate closes."

"I'll make it for you," our driver replies, a serious expression on his face. "You just need to trust me and not worry."

His determination gives me hope. If he believes that it is going to be possible to get us to the airport in time, then maybe it is. He has been driving tourists to and from the airport for years. I am, in a way, in the best of hands. We head to a restaurant, where Mark and Dad eat some chapatti bread, potatoes, and chicken. I still cannot stomach anything. We stay for only an hour before I haul everyone back into the car.

"It is almost ready," I am told when we walk back into the immigration office. Twenty-five minutes later the officer hurries back to us. "Please sign here. And initial here." He rushes out of sight, reappearing a few minutes later with the final copy. He places it in my hand.

"Go."

Without pausing even to glance at the paper, I swing Mark up into my arms and we rush for the exit. Our driver sees us running toward him and hurries to open the passenger doors. He has the car beginning to move even before we are fully inside.

For once I am appreciative of Africa's unorthodox driving methods as we swerve in and out of lanes, blasting the horn to alert other drivers to move. Our flight is scheduled to depart in an hour and a half. The car constantly bumps and swerves along the road, and I can't help but compare it to the winding adventure that has been my life for the past three years. Now at the end of this extraordinary story, when I look back on all that has transpired, all that God miraculously orchestrated, I find it almost difficult to believe that I questioned so many times whether God would see this through. I am closing the chapter on adoption paperwork and government bureaucracy, and beginning a new story in which Mark and I will be a family forever.

Never will I forget the miracles God performed to keep Mark and me together, nor how he faithfully sustained me through my fears and my doubts. I encountered many moments of despair when I was tempted to believe it all depended on me and that the outcome of the adoption rested in my hands alone. Yet time and time again, Jesus, in his great mercy, strengthened me with the truth that he is sovereign. I know for certain that this story is not just about me and Mark, but is, rather, part of a larger story about God and his faithfulness.

I look down at Mark. He is struggling to keep his eyes open and leans his head on my shoulder. His little hands are wrapped around my forearm. Trying not to disturb him, I reach into the folder where I frantically shoved the paper from immigration. I pull it out and stare at it for the first time. *Mark Kirab Swann. Confirmation of Permanent Residence.*

"We are going home, sweetie," I whisper ever so softly as I lean down and gently kiss him on the head. "You and I are going home."

EPILOGUE

FOLLOWING THE finalization of the adoption, Mark and I returned to Calgary, where I decided to pursue my Master's in Clinical Social Work. For years Mark prayed for a father and sibling, and in early 2010 Mark's prayers were answered when I married a wonderful Colombian man of God, Carlos Castilla. We welcomed our second son, Uzziah Levi, into our family at the end of that year. Mark's second brother, Rafayel Ezra, joined the family in the summer of 2013.

I worked for a number of years in forensic mental health with youth, but have recently taken on the role as the new Program Director at Christian Adoption Services in Alberta.

MARK KIRAB, NOW eleven years old, is in the sixth grade. He is an extremely gentle and caring boy, always looking out for others and very protective of the ones he loves. He is a wonderful and patient big brother, and his little siblings look up to him and adore him. He is very well liked by his peers as he is easygoing, laughs readily, and is always described as "very polite and kind." Rather than using his chore/allowance money on himself, Mark decided to put it toward sponsoring a child in Colombia.

Physically, Mark is tall, strong, athletic, and perfectly healthy. He loves to be outside and plays all kinds of sports. He especially loves hockey and soccer. He is also naturally gifted at music, especially with rhythm. Mark currently plays the drums and is very talented at all kinds of different dancing styles. God has gifted him in so many ways, and he is truly a blessing to his family and to those around him.

Tandela Castilla
October 2014

*Tandy and Mark in December 2006, after receiving the adoption
authorization letter from the Soroti High Court.*

*Castilla Family in 2013:
Uzziah, Carlos, Mark, Tandela, and Rafayel.*

ACKNOWLEDGMENTS

Tandy: Thank you for your heroic efforts in your faithfulness to God's call. I am profoundly grateful for your grace and patience over the last five years as I have laboured, often clumsily, to write your and Mark's story. I treasure beyond words the gift of you opening up and entrusting your heart to me. Mark, thank you for always welcoming me with a bright smile when I came to Calgary, even though it meant I would be pestering your mom with questions throughout my visit. Carlos, thank you also for trusting me with your wife's story, of which God always knew you would be a part.

The Swann Family: I first met you all when you opened up your home to me thirteen years ago. David and Laureen, you have always been incredibly hospitable and generous, and I cannot thank you enough for your support in this project and for taking the time to share your part in the story. Nathan Swann and Kirsten Archuleta, thank you also for your vulnerability in our interviews and for your kindness. David and Kirsten, I am very appreciative of your encouraging feedback on previous drafts of the manuscript.

Sharon Nyanjura, you were a source of great strength and encouragement to Tandy. I thank you for your friendship to her, and for your hospitality to me and Aaron in Uganda. You are doing wonderful work there.

Thank you to those friends and family who, year after year, continually asked how the writing was going. In particular I would like to thank Laura Colley, Lana Muller, Jen Por, and Karla Bretherick for your thoughtful feedback on previous drafts. Along with the four of you, I would like to thank the many others at Westside Church who have prayed with and for me at various times throughout the years in my struggle to complete this work. Thank you for your steadfastness in your own stories; you are a constant source of encouragement to me.

I also extend my gratitude to Rebecca Wigod who provided me with very helpful information regarding the publishing industry, and to both Rebecca and Holly Horwood for your valuable feedback on a particular chapter of the book. Jon Imbeau, thank you for meeting with me to share of your experiences in Uganda.

Gary and Barbara Rose, thank you for your constant support and careful reads of a previous draft. Barbara, stories of your faithfulness to God's call would fill many pages.

My parents, Edward and Diana Safarik: I am incredibly appreciative of your efforts in helping to bring this book to completion. Thank you for all the times you happily looked after Owen, especially during our trip to Uganda. I will be forever grateful for your demonstration of love to me, and for teaching me what it means to be loved. Bryan and Amanda, I am indebted to you for the time you have generously given to Owen and Charlie. Jacob, thank you for your thoughtful feedback on earlier portions of the book.

My dear friend and editor, Keri Haywood, principal editor at Sui Generis Editing: You were first my friend and then became an answer to prayer as God chose you to be my editor. Your talents have made this book into something it would never have been on its own. Thank you for your tremendous investment in this project and for not being afraid to push me to where I didn't know I could go. And to Ariana Bissky of True Story Editing & Design for your help in copy editing and laying out the book. You are excellent at what you do and give beautiful attention to detail. I am very appreciative of your helpful feedback on previous drafts and for your meticulous proofing of the final copy.

Owen, Charlie, and Lucy, you are still wee little things, but without you I would never be able to understand Tandy's love for Mark and write from the perspective of a mother. With you as my children I have a greater understanding of God as my Heavenly Father. Thank you for this.

To my husband and helpmate Aaron: You have prayed more than anyone else for this project. Thank you for your words of encouragement, for listening to all my doubts and fears, for holding my hand through the tears and celebrating the milestones. You have been my constant sounding board, patiently helping me when I couldn't find the right words or when a sentence didn't read well. We never knew what this would turn out to be, and yet you never hesitated giving of your time and talents to see it through. Thank you also for willingly accompanying me to Uganda when it meant we would have to leave our eleven-month-old son at home. Yet far beyond all of these things, I am grateful to God for your character, one that is founded on your love for Jesus. Aside from knowing him and his Word, I count our marriage as God's greatest gift to me.

Jesus, you are the author of this story and all stories. If there is anything of worth on these pages, anything that can bring encouragement or joy, it is because of your Almighty hand. This is a love story of a mother's love for her son, and yet it is so much more. It is the story of your love for us, and for the world. Thank you for inviting us into your story, and for the hope that you offer through your life, death, and resurrection.

RESOURCES

To learn more about adoption, caring for orphans, or how to help the poor and vulnerable in Uganda, please check out these great resources:

Arise and Shine Uganda

www.ariseandshineuganda.com

Arise and Shine Uganda is the fulfillment of the goal of Tandy's friend Sharon Nyanjura, featured in this book, to found a non-profit to support local children and families through income-generation projects, education, support outreach, and a children's home specifically for vulnerable and abandoned infants, many of whom are disabled. One of the ways to support AASU is by sponsoring a child.

Amazima Ministries

www.amazima.org

Amazima Ministries works to empower and educate the people of Uganda through God's love. Specifically, Amazima provides daily meals to over a thousand vulnerable children from a slum community, offers medical care and education to hundreds of children from extremely poor families around Jinja, and equips Ugandan farmers with sustainable and profitable methods for farming. There are a variety of ways to help Amazima, including sponsoring a child.

JENGA Uganda
www.jengauganda.org

JENGA is a local Uganda organization that is focused on the poorest communities in Mbale. JENGA trains local farmers, empowers widows to generate income through the breeding and selling of goats, provides food for orphaned and malnourished children as well as paying for their school fees and uniforms, and is also focused on providing health care and clean water to the Mbale community.

The Lulu Tree
www.thelulutree.com

The Lulu Tree's vision is "Preventing tomorrow's orphans by equipping today's mothers." They seek to accomplish this through their two-year mama sponsorship program. The goal, by the end of the two years, is for each mama to be self-sufficient as she cares for her children, pursues her dreams, and ends the cycle of poverty for her family—all in the name and hope of Jesus Christ. They work primarily in the slums of Kampala, Uganda.

ABBA Canada

www.abbacanada.com

ABBA Canada helps with the financial burden of adoption by providing loans and grants to families hoping to adopt. It also focuses on equipping and empowering local churches to support and meet the needs of adoptive families.

The ABBA Fund

www.abbafund.org

The ABBA Fund provides interest-free adoption loans and grant funds to families. Its website offers a wealth of helpful adoption-related information.

Christian Adoption Services

www.christianadoption.ab.ca

CAS supports families through both domestic and international adoptions and provides support and counseling to expectant/birth parents.